Computer & Internet Dictionary

for Ages 9 to 99

By Charles W. Berry and William H. Hawn, Jr.

Illustrated by Yvette Santiago Banek
and Denise Gilgannon

BARRON'S

All inquiries should be addressed to:
Barron's Educational Series, Inc.
250 Wireless Boulevard
Hauppauge, New York 11788
http://www.barronseduc.com

International Standard Book No.: 0-7641-1520-0

Library of Congress Catalog Card No. 00-037852

Library of Congress Cataloging-in-Publication Data
Berry, Charles W.
    Computer and Internet dictionary for ages 9 to 99 / Charles W. Berry and
William H. Hawn, Jr. ; illustrated by Yvette Santiago Banek and Denise Gilgannon.
      p. cm.
    Summary: Defines over eight hundred computer and Internet terms.
    ISBN 0-7641-1520-0
      1. Internet (Computer network)—Dictionaries. 2. Computers—Dictionaries.
[1. Internet (Computer network)—Dictionaries. 2. Computers—Dictionaries.]
I. Hawn, William H. II. Banek, Yvette Santiago, ill. III. Title.

TK5105.875.I57 S556   2000
004′.03—dc21   00-037852

Printed in Hong Kong

9 8 7 6 5 4 3 2 1

Dedication

For Jada, Robin, and little Juan
C. W. B.

For Evan
W. H. H.

Acknowledgments

he authors wish to thank Jay Kluborg, Joy Hawn, and Jennifer K. Watkins for their many useful comments and suggestions.

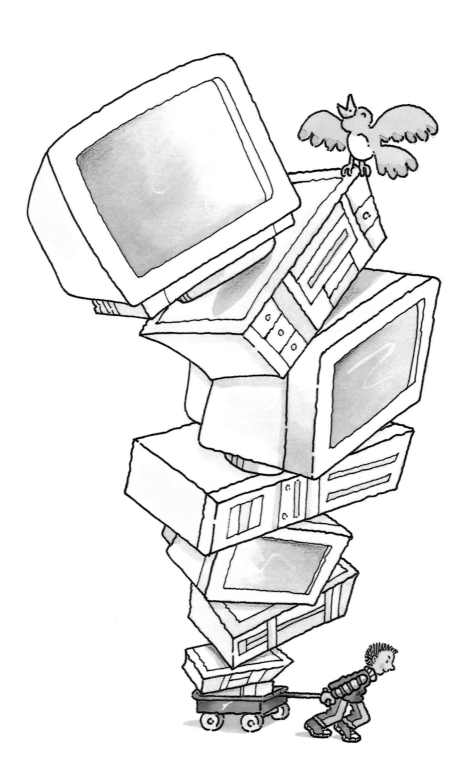

TABLE OF CONTENTS

Introduction

Only 15 years ago, people did not send e-mail or use the Internet. Today, laptop computers are popping up everywhere. Very soon, even refrigerators and toasters may have computer chips inside them and be linked to the Internet. In the near future, many things that you do for work or for play may have to do with computers and the Internet. So, understanding computers and the Internet is important. To do so, you have to know the words that people use when they use computers and the Internet, either for work or for play.

Think of something that you like to do. Do you play a musical instrument? Do you have a dog or a cat that you feed and care for? Do you play sports? If you had to explain any of these activities to an alien visiting Earth for the first time, you would have to explain what the words mean. "What is a *dog*?" or "What is a *baseball*?" your new alien friend would ask. Just as the alien visitor would have to know the meanings of your words to understand your hobbies and interests, so must you understand the meanings of computer and Internet words to use computers and the Internet.

A Special Note for Parents

Today, children have access to computers and the Internet. The power of these tools was beyond belief only a few decades ago. Some people use computers to make better use of their time, and others use computers as a hobby. We all use computers every day, whether we know it or not. Computers help to manage inventory in grocery stores, regulate the combustion in our cars, deliver electric power to our homes, and let us call our loved ones on the telephone. This book gives your children the opportunity to learn the vocabulary needed to use computers and the Internet. It also gives you the opportunity to brush up on your computer and Internet know-how and to help your children learn.

The Internet is a tool that gives your children access to an amazing variety of information. Like all tools, it can be used for good or for ill. As your children use the Internet, you should monitor them to be sure that they avoid harmful material.

The Internet contains an amazingly wide spectrum of information and opinions. Not all of it is valid, however. Work with your children so that they understand that any information obtained through the Internet (or any source) must be carefully considered for its validity. Let the Internet become an opportunity to teach your children critical thinking. This, after all, will be one of the most important skills that they will need in the twenty-first century. Help your children to understand that they are responsible for the way in which they use computers and the Internet and that they must make wise decisions.

How to Use This Book

This book contains the definitions of over 845 computer and Internet terms. The appendix lists abbreviations used in informal e-mail, chat, and Usenet.

You can use the definitions any time you need to know what a term means. You can also read the definitions for fun and to learn about computers and the Internet. However you choose to learn, good luck on your journey!

....

The order of terms

Terms beginning with symbols appear first, in the section "Symbols and Numbers." Terms are alphabetized letter by letter, ignoring spaces, hyphens, and forward slashes. Symbols and numbers come before letters.

....

Easy guide to related words

For some words, you will want to read the definitions of other words. Look for the Look up eye, 👁 . The Look up eye will guide you to related words that you may also want to know about. Also, some terms have the same meaning as other terms. For these terms, the Look up eye will guide you to the term that is standard. For example,

star 👁 Look up *asterisk.*

Computer terms can have more than one meaning.

Some computer terms have more than one meaning. When a term has more than one definition, a (1) will be assigned to the first definition and a (2) will be assigned to the second definition. When you see these numbers in a definition, you will know that the term can be used in more than one way.

Some definitions are for PCs. Some are for Macs.

Most, but not all, computer terms apply to all computers. Some terms only apply to PCs; others only apply to Macs. In this book, there is a way to tell if a definition is for PCs or Macs.

Terms in the color blue apply only to IBM and IBM-compatible computers.

Terms in the color red apply only to Macintosh computers.

PC and Mac keyboards are on page 5. You can look at these drawings whenever a key is mentioned in a definition.

For thousands of years, humans have computed, recorded facts, communicated information, and expressed themselves. Ancient artifacts show evidence of computing and record keeping. Humans have talked with each other for so long that no one is exactly sure when and where talking began. The walls of the caves of Lascaux, France, and many other sites are filled with drawings made by ancient peoples. No one is sure exactly what these drawings mean. However, one thing is certain: the ancient people were *expressing* themselves. No wonder, then, that computers and the Internet are so important to us. Computers and the Internet, after all, let us compute, keep records, communicate, and express ourselves but in ways that were never before imagined.

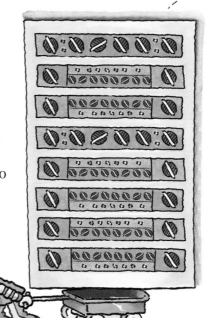

Early computing devices were used for computation. Computers also played an important role in World War II, where they were used to encode and decode messages. In the late 1960s, computer scientists discovered ways to make computers talk with each other. They began work on a network that scientists could use to communicate about their work.

The 1970s was an important decade in computers. In the early 1970s, the first computer network was up and running. It linked about two dozen research centers.

The first truly personal computer became available in the mid-1970s. This computer was called the Apple I. It was actually a kit that hobbyists could buy. You had to build it yourself! Later, the Apple II was invented. It was a completely assembled computer. In the mid-1980s, Apple introduced the Macintosh, and IBM also introduced a personal computer.

Also in the 1980s, government and university research laboratories formed the ARPANET. While this system provided the conceptual basis for the Internet, the ARPANET was not available to the public.

The early 1990s saw the introduction of computer networks to the public. Now, at the beginning of the twenty-first century, people from all over the world can travel the information super-highway. As of this writing, the World Wide Web contains over 70,000,000 web sites, and the number is growing.

You may be wondering what the Internet, which so many people are talking about, has to offer to you. The answer, simply put, is that it may have more things than anyone could possibly imagine to offer to you. In what other single place could you find information about your favorite president or the latest news and sports or shop for toys? The Internet makes your computer such a place.

What exactly is the Internet? The Internet is a vast network of computer networks and all the content that can be delivered through the system. The Internet allows e-mail, online discussions, and a virtual library of information and opinions from all over the world.

What can you do on the Internet? It is tempting to say "everything!" The Internet links you to facts and lets you communicate and share information with people all over the world. If you like sports, you can find a web site about sports. If you like art,

you can find a web site about art—almost anything you can think of has a web site! Here is a list of things that you can do on the Internet:

- Learn about the world.
- Communicate with people far away.
- Learn about a subject so that you can do well in school.

- Learn about what is going on in the world. Whether an earthquake strikes somewhere in the world or NASA finds a new planet orbiting a star, you can find something about it on the Internet.

- Learn about events when they happen. The Internet allows you to learn what is happening in a special area as soon as it is reported. All you have to do is enter the words and/or phrases that you want to find out about.

- Make a difference in the way the people of the world understand themselves and each other. Today, people can communicate with others who live in countries that share a common language. One day soon, perhaps, people will be able to talk through translating devices to anyone with a computer. When this is possible, the people of the world will learn what their differences and similarities are. From this, they may discover that they share the same hopes. The dream of a peaceful, cooperative world may become real.

....

How to Access the Internet

Anyone with a telephone, cable, or wireless connection and a computer can use the Internet. You may have a connection at home, or you may use a computer at a library that is connected to the Internet. Remember, though, to ask permission to use someone else's connection, even if you know the password. Connections can be temporary or permanent. Most connections from home are temporary and are achieved by using a modem to dial an Internet service provider.

PC keyboard layout

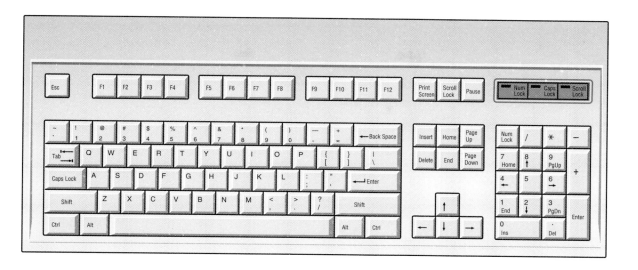

Macintosh keyboard layout

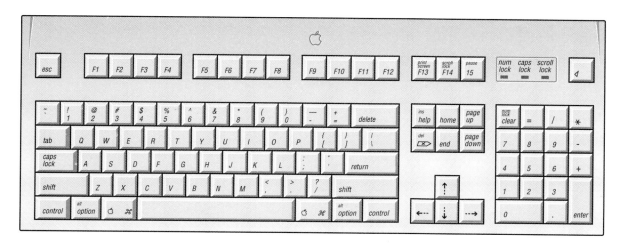

? Symbols & Numbers

 The *apple symbol* is the symbol of Apple Computer, Incorporated. The apple symbol is also the icon for the Apple menu on Apple computers. Look up *Apple menu*.

* An *asterisk* (*) is a star-shaped symbol. Six different styles of asterisks appear below.

(1) In DOS, Windows, OS/2, and UNIX, an asterisk is a wild card. When you want to use a file but are not sure about its file name, you can use an asterisk to replace one or all of the letters in the file name or in the file name extension. For example, *.exe means all the files that end in .exe (the DOS command for finding these files is dir*.exe). Look up *DOS, extension, OS/2, UNIX, wild card,* and *Windows*.
(2) When an asterisk appears next to a word, it means that more facts about that word will be found at the bottom of the page. These additional facts are called footnotes.

¦ The *pipe* (¦) is a symbol on your keyboard. It is on the backslash key (shift-backslash). Pipe commands work in MS-DOS and UNIX systems. A pipe is typically used to connect two commands so that the output from the first command becomes input for the second command. For example, to display files in sorted order, enter DIR|SORT. Look up *backslash, command, MS-DOS,* and *UNIX*.

? The question mark symbol ? is a wild card that stands for a single character. For example, if you type dir a?c, the computer will return files named abc, amc, azc, or any other file whose name has three letters and begins with an *a* and ends with a *c*. Look up *character* and *wild card*.

3-D rendering The things a computer does to turn instructions into a picture that looks like it has height, width, and depth on a computer monitor are called *3-D rendering*. Most computer images have only height and width. 3-D rendering is done automatically by VRML viewers. Look up *image, monitor, ray tracing,* and *VRML*.

3½-inch diskette Look up *diskette*.

3.5-inch diskette Look up *diskette*.

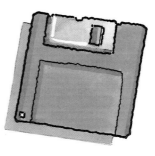

5¼-inch diskette A *5¼-inch diskette* is an older kind of diskette. 5¼-inch diskettes were the first diskettes used in personal computers. They are not commonly used anymore. ◉ Look up *diskette.*

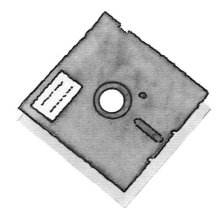

8-bit microprocessor A bit is a tiny piece of information, a 0 or a 1. An *8-bit microprocessor* is a processor that handles 8 bits of information at a time. Some of the earliest computers had 8-bit microprocessors. These computers were slow by today's standards because they contained simple instructions. ◉ Look up *bit, information,* and *microprocessor.*

16-bit graphics *16-bit graphics* is a color system that allows 65,536 different colors to be displayed on your computer's monitor. 16-bit graphics uses 16 bits for each pixel. 16-bit graphics is used to approximate 24-bit graphics and allows realistic images. Trees look like real trees, and people look like real people. ◉ Look up *24-bit graphics, bit,* and *monitor.*

16-bit microprocessor A bit is a tiny piece of information, a 0 or a 1. A *16-bit microprocessor* is a microprocessor that processes 16 bits of information at a time. A 16-bit microprocessor is often faster and more powerful than an 8-bit microprocessor because it can process more complicated instructions. ◉ Look up *bit, information,* and *microprocessor.*

24-bit graphics *24-bit graphics* is a color system that allows millions of colors to be displayed on your computer's monitor. 24-bit graphics uses 24 bits for each pixel, so 16,777,216 colors are possible. 24-bit graphics is also known as true color because this mode allows realistic images. Trees look like real trees, and people look like real people. ◉ Look up *16-bit graphics, bit,* and *monitor.*

32-bit microprocessor A bit is a tiny piece of information, a 0 or a 1. A *32-bit microprocessor* is a microprocessor that processes 32 bits of information at a time. The instructions can be more complicated and it can work with more complicated kinds of data than a 16-bit microprocessor. Also, it can use greater amounts of memory more easily than simpler microprocessors. ◉ Look up *bit* and *microprocessor.*

386 The *386* microprocessor was a microprocessor used in IBM PCs. It was a 32-bit microprocessor. The 386 was capable of multitasking, which means that it could run more than one program at once. ◉ Look up *32-bit microprocessor, microprocessor, multitasking,* and *program.*

....

56k modem A *56k modem* is a modem that can transfer data at the rate of 56,000 bits per second. Before the development of DSL, this was the speed limit for data being sent by telephone. ◉ Look up *data, DSL,* and *modem.*

....

8088 The *8088* microprocessor was the microprocessor used in the first IBM PCs. ◉ Look up *microprocessor* and *PC.*

....

68000 The *68000* microprocessor was the microprocessor in the original Macintosh computer. ◉ Look up *Macintosh* and *microprocessor.*

....

68020 The 68000 line of microprocessors were the microprocessors used in the Macintosh computers before the PowerPC CPU. The *68020* microprocessor was an improvement on the 68000 microprocessor. ◉ Look up *68000, CPU, Macintosh, microprocessor,* and *PowerPC CPU.*

....

68030 The 68000 line of microprocessors were the microprocessors used in the Macintosh computers before the PowerPC CPU. The *68030* microprocessor was an improvement on the 68020 microprocessor. ◉ Look up *CPU, Macintosh, microprocessor,* and *PowerPC CPU.*

....

AAMOF *AAMOF* is an abbreviation for "as a matter of fact." It is used in informal e-mail, chat, and Usenet.

> *Mary: Are you ready for the dance recital?*
> *Juan:* **aamof***, I practiced for six hours yesterday.*

See the appendix, pages 189–190, for a complete table of abbreviations. 👁 Look up *chat, e-mail,* and *Usenet.*

abort *Abort* means to stop something you are doing on a computer. You may be playing a computer game, writing an e-mail to a friend or to your grandmother, or saving a file. If you stop before you are finished, you abort whatever it is you are doing. Many programs offer you a chance to abort an instruction to your computer if that instruction will cause you to lose work or data. There is usually a special abort key for this, or you may use the mouse.

> *John was about to erase a word processor file when he remembered that there was a poem on it that Mary liked. He* **aborted** *the deletion so that she could make a copy.*

👁 Look up *e-mail, file, mouse, save,* and *word processor.*

accelerator An *accelerator* is a device that makes an operation run faster. For example, a graphics accelerator is a card that has built-in circuits for performing graphics operations. Using this card allows your computer to work with the graphics more quickly. 👁 Look up *circuit, graphics,* and *PC card.*

accents Marks added to letters (as in ë, é, ê, è) to show differences in pronunciation. Most computer software treats a letter with an accent as a single character. 👁 Look up *software.*

acceptable use policy *Acceptable use policy* is a set of rules established by an Internet service provider concerning acceptable use of the network. Rules should cover types of behavior that will not be allowed on the network and the penalties for breaking these rules. 👁 Look up *access provider* and *Internet service provider.*

access **(1)** If you are able to get information from a computer, a disk, or a web site, you have *access.* 👁 Look up *computer, disk, information,* and *web site.*
(2) *Access* is the process of retrieving data from RAM, a storage device, or a network. 👁 Look up *CD-ROM, CPU, floppy disk, hard disk, RAM,* and *storage device.*

access code An *access code* is a group of letters and/or symbols that you use to start a computer or enter a web site. An access code is also called a password. 👁 Look up *password* and *web site.*

---

access provider A company that provides its customers with access to the Internet is an *access provider.* Major access providers in the United States include America Online, Microsoft, Mindspring, and Netcom. The customer usually pays a monthly fee and the access provider supplies software that enables the customer to connect to the Internet by modem.

---

access speed *Access speed* is the speed at which information can travel from one location to another. 👁 Look up *access time* and *baud rate.*

---

access time *Access time* is how fast your computer's CPU can begin to transfer information to the cache, memory, a storage device, or a computer network. Your computer's RAM has the fastest access time because the information has to travel over only a circuit, and it can do that very quickly. When you flip a light switch, the light comes on almost at the same time. A computer can access memory at least that fast! The access speed for a hard disk or floppy disk is slower but still fast. CD-ROMs have the slowest access speeds. 👁 Look up *cache, circuit, CPU, floppy disk, hard disk, information,* and *RAM.*

---

accessibility **(1)** If you have *accessibility* to a computer, program, or web site, then you are able to use the computer, program, or Web site.

(2) *Accessibility* refers to how easy a computer, a program, or a web site is to use. For example, a site accessible by only experts using a special browser has poor accessibility, while a web site that can be viewed by any browser has good accessibility. 👁 Look up *browser, program,* and *web site.*

ACM *ACM* is an abbreviation for Association for Computing Machinery. ACM is a worldwide association of computer professionals. Their web address is *www.acm.org.*

---

acronym An *acronym* is a word made from letters from a word or phrase. A boy named Robert Jackson may go by R. J. Acronyms are similar. RAM is an acronym. It stands for **r**andom-**a**ccess **m**emory. The word LAN is another acronym. It stands for **l**ocal-**a**rea **n**etwork:

Local-Area Network
↓
L = Local   A = Area   N = Network
↓
LAN

Initials for human names, such as R. J., use the first letter of each name. Acronyms for computer terms, on the other hand, sometimes use more than just the first letter of a word and sometimes skip all the letters of a word. For example, ISOC stands for **I**nternet **S**ociety, and LAPM stands for **l**ink **a**ccess **p**rotocol for **m**odems.

Why are acronyms used? Just like an abbreviation, acronyms give people an easy way to refer to longer words and groups of words. They also make reading easier because an acronym can take the place of several words. For example, instead of saying or writing, "The central processing unit receives data from random access memory," you can just say or write, "The CPU receives data from RAM." 👁 Look up *CPU, data,* and *RAM.*

activate (1) You *activate* the window in which you want to type by moving the mouse pointer into the window and clicking or clicking on the window's title bar.

(2) You *activate* a piece of software by double-clicking on its name or icon. 👁 Look up *icon, mouse pointer,* and *window.*

active A menu item or feature is *active* if you can use it. For example, menu items

that you can select and use are active, while items that you cannot use are inactive. Inactive items usually appear in a lighter color from that of active items so that you will know they are inactive. 👁 Look up *inactive* and *menu.*

active color An *active color* is the color you have selected in a paint or draw program. The tool being used will paint or draw in the active color. 👁 Look up *draw program* and *paint program.*

active window An *active window* is the window in which the user is typing, drawing, or making menu choices. 👁 Look up *activate, menu,* and *window.*

actor In an animation program, the *actor* is an object that moves in a specified way along a path, or line. 👁 Look up *animation* and *program.*

adaptive technology *Adaptive technology* helps people with physical limitations. Computer-related adaptive devices include magnified screen displays, speech recognition devices, and special keyboards for people who can only press one key at a time. 👁 Look up *device, keyboard,* and *speech recognition.*

ADB *ADB* is an abbreviation for **A**pple **D**esk-top **B**us. 👁 Look up *Apple Desktop Bus.*

adventure game An *adventure game* is a computer game in which the player finds a path through a set of screens, where each screen represents a room or stage along the path. The player has to reach a goal, such as reaching the final screen, in order to have mastered the game. ◉ Look up *virtual reality.*

adware Software that is distributed free as a form of advertising is known as *adware.*

AFAIK *AFAIK* is an abbreviation for "as far as I know." It is used in informal e-mail, chat, and Usenet.

> Paul: *Where's the party?*
> John: *The party's at Mark's at 7:00 P.M.,* ***afaik***.

See the appendix, pages 189–190, for a complete table of abbreviations. ◉ Look up *chat, e-mail,* and *Usenet.*

AFAIR *AFAIR* is an abbreviation for "as far as I remember." It is used in informal e-mail, chat, and Usenet.

> Paul: *I think we are supposed to work the problems for Section 6 for tomorrow,* ***afair***.
> Mary: *OK.*

See the appendix, pages 189–190, for a complete table of abbreviations. ◉ Look up *chat, e-mail,* and *Usenet.*

AFK *AFK* is an abbreviation for "away from keyboard." It is used in informal e-mail, chat, and Usenet.

> ***afk***. *I'll be back online tonight.*

See the appendix, pages 189–190, for a complete table of abbreviations. ◉ Look up *chat, e-mail,* and *Usenet.*

AI *AI* is an acronym for **a**rtificial **i**ntelligence. ◉ Look up *artificial intelligence.*

AIFF *AIFF* is an abbreviation for **A**udio **I**nterchange **F**ile **F**ormat. AIFF files are audio files that you can play. Many web sites have AIFF files that you can download. ◉ Look up *audio, download, file,* and *Web site.*

airbrush An *airbrush* is a tool available in some paint programs that allows the user to make edges soft and colors translucent.

alert box An *alert box* is a small window that appears to give the user information. Usually the user has to click on a button to make the box disappear. 👁 Look up *message box.*

algorithm An *algorithm* is a set of instructions for doing something. Here is an algorithm for making a banana split.

1. **Peel and slice a banana.**
2. **Put the banana slices into a dish.**
3. **Add ice cream.**
4. **Add fruit and flavored syrup.**
5. **Add whipped cream and a cherry on top.**

Computers follow algorithms when they operate, but the algorithms that they follow are much more complicated than the algorithm for making a banana split!

alias On Macintosh computers, an *alias* is an icon that lets you easily open a file, a folder, or a disk. You can also use an alias to start a program. Windows computers have a similar feature, called a shortcut. 👁 Look up *disk, file, folder, icon, Macintosh, program, shortcut,* and *Windows.*

align To *align* objects or text is to make them line up, either horizontally or vertically. Most draw programs and page layout programs have specific commands to help you align objects and text.

Alta Vista *Alta Vista* is a World Wide Web search engine. 👁 Look up *search engine* and *World Wide Web.*

alpha testing Everyone has had to take tests in school. These tests show the teacher whether you know what you are

supposed to know and if you can do things as you should. Computer software, such as video games, word processors, and so on, must be tested so that programmers can know if they will work properly. *Alpha testing* is the first step in testing software. Alpha testing is named after alpha (a), the first letter in the Greek alphabet. The next two steps are beta testing and gamma testing. 👁 Look up *beta testing, gamma testing, Greek alphabet, programmer, software,* and *word processor.*

alphanumeric Information that contains only letters and numbers is *alphanumeric* information.

ABCDE+12345

Alt key The *Alt key* is a special key on PC computers, a modifier key. You hold down the Alt key while pressing another key to do a special operation or to make a special character. 👁 Look up *modifier key.*

Amazon.com *Amazon.com* is an online bookstore. Customers buy books through the World Wide Web. 👁 Look up *World Wide Web* and *online.*

ambient lighting *Ambient lighting* is lighting that is all around an object.

Ambient lighting is very often natural lighting from a source, such as the sun. Ambient lighting is not directed at any specific object.

ambient temperature The temperature in the area around something, like the air temperature in a room or the water temperature in a fish bowl, is the *ambient temperature.*

America Online (AOL) *America Online* is an online information service that offers its subscribers Internet access and e-mail, among other services. 👁 Look up *e-mail* and *Internet.*

ampersand An *ampersand* is the character &. It stands for the word *and.*

analog A device is *analog* when it operates by a range of electric values, not just the two electric on and off states. 👁 Look up *device.*

android An *android* is a machine, or robot, that looks like a person. The difference between a person and an android is that an android has a computer for a brain and a body made of artificial materials. Currently, androids are found only in fiction. Someday, androids may take the place of waiters. 👁 Look up *machine* and *robot.*

angle brackets Angle brackets are the characters < >.

animated GIF An *animated GIF* is a kind of movie that you can download from a web site or some other source and watch. 👁 Look up *download, GIF,* and *web site.*

animation A computer *animation* is a computer-made image that changes as you watch it. Computer animations are made by displaying slightly different images one by one. Older computers were too slow to produce good animation, but today computers can make great animations. You will see many animations when you use computers and the Internet. For example, most video games are animated in some way. Also, the World Wide Web is filled with animations.

Can I make animations? Yes. A number of programs let you make your own animations. A fun way to make animations and to understand how computers make animations is to draw images on a stack of index cards. Draw pictures on the index cards and make each new image a little different from the last image. When you flip through the cards quickly, you will see your animation come to life! 👁 Look up *Internet* and *World Wide Web.*

antivirus program An *antivirus program* is a program that can find viruses and destroy them. Most antivirus programs run automatic scans of memory, disks, and files that you download. Antivirus programs must be updated from time to time so that they can handle new viruses that are created. Updating can often be done over the Internet. 👁 Look up *disk, download, file, Internet, memory,* and *virus.*

antistatic mat Static electricity can damage your computer. An *antistatic mat* is a

mat that protects your computer from the buildup of static electricity.

AOL 👁 Look up *America Online.*

Apple Computer, Incorporated *Apple Computer, Incorporated* is one of the most important companies in computing. It was founded by Steve Wozniak and Steve Jobs. Apple Computer makes the iMac, iBook, Powerbook, PowerMac, and other computers. Apple Computer's Apple II, which was introduced in 1977, was the first widely available personal computer.

The Macintosh line of computers was introduced in 1984 and was the first line of personal computers available with a graphical user interface (GUI). 👁 Look up *graphical user interface; iBook; iMac; Jobs, Stephen; Power PC; Wozniak, Stephen.*

Apple Desktop Bus (ADB) If you have a Macintosh computer, the *Apple Desktop Bus* is the system that lets your keyboard, mouse, and other input devices work. 👁 Look up *keyboard, input device,* and *mouse.*

Apple menu The *Apple menu* is a special menu on Macintosh computers. It holds desk accessories, the control panel, and aliases of files. 👁 Look up *alias, control panel,* and *Macintosh.*

applet An *applet* is a small program. For example, the simple calculators and simple video games that may be on your computer are applets. Applets are also downloaded to your computer when you view web pages using your web browser. Applets are usually written in Java. 👁 Look up *download, Java, web browser,* and *web page.*

AppleTalk *AppleTalk* is the network built into Macintosh computers and peripherals. AppleTalk lets Macintosh computers communicate with each other and with devices such as printers. Macintosh computers linked by AppleTalk are an example of a LAN. 👁 Look up *communicate, device, LAN, printer,* and *Macintosh.*

application program A program that lets you do something with your computer is an *application program.* For example, video games and word processors are application programs.

Are all programs application programs? No. Programs that do something for your computer are not application programs. For example, a data compression program is not an application program. 👁 Look up *data compression, program, utility program,* and *word processor.*

application programmer An *application programmer* is a person who writes programs that allow your computer to do something useful or fun. Video games, word processors, and spreadsheets are

examples of the kinds of programs that application programmers write. 👁 Look up *spreadsheet* and *word processor.*

....

application programming *Application programming* is the work that an application programmer does, such as writing video games, word processors, and spreadsheets. 👁 Look up *application programmer, spreadsheet, video game,* and *word processor.*

....

application shortcut An *application shortcut* is a file that lets you launch an application program. Application shortcuts can be icons on the desktop or items in a menu. 👁 Look up *application program* and *launch.*

....

application window When you use an application, one window is usually always open in which you do the most important work. This window is the *application window.* 👁 Look up *window.*

....

arrow keys *Arrow keys* are keys on your keyboard that let you move the cursor up and down and side to side. 👁 Look up *cursor* and *keyboard.*

....

artificial intelligence (AI) You are intelligent. Computers, on the other hand, are not intelligent, even though they can do some amazing things. Intelligence is about

thinking, understanding, relating, and creating—all of the things that humans do every day. Computers store and retrieve data, calculate, and display information, but they are not usually considered intelligent. Some people want to make computers that can do all of these things. They want to make computers with *artificial intelligence.* 👁 Look up *computer, data,* and *retrieve.*

....

ASAP *ASAP* is an acronym for **as s**oon **as p**ossible.

> *"Please hand in your homework ASAP,"* John's teacher said.

....

ascender An *ascender* is the part of the lowercase letters *b, d, f, h, k, l,* and *t* that reach above the height of letters like *x* and *u.* 👁 Look up *descender* and *lowercase.*

Rubber baby buggy bumpers

....

ascending order *Ascending order* is a way of listing items so that the smallest is first, the largest is last, and each item in the list is larger than the item before it. For example, 0, 1, 2, 3, 4, 5, 6, 7, 8, 9, is a list in ascending order.

....

ASCII *ASCII* is an abbreviation for **A**merican **S**tandard **C**ode for **I**nformation **I**nterchange. Letters of the alphabet, like *A, B, C,* and all the other simple characters

ASCII

ASCII code	Character	ASCII code	Character	ASCII code	Character	ASCII code	Character	ASCII code	Character
0	Ctrl-@	27	Ctrl-\	54	6	81	Q	108	l
1	Ctrl-A	28	Ctrl-/	55	7	82	R	109	m
2	Ctrl-B	29	Ctrl-]	56	8	83	S	110	n
3	Ctrl-C	30	Ctrl-~	57	9	84	T	111	o
4	Ctrl-D	31	Ctrl-_	58	:	85	U	112	p
5	Ctrl-E	32	Space	59	;	86	V	113	q
6	Ctrl-F	33	!	60	<	87	W	114	r
7	Ctrl-G	34	"	61	=	88	X	115	s
8	Backspace	35	#	62	>	89	Y	116	t
9	Tab	36	$	63	?	90	Z	117	u
10	Ctrl-J	37	%	64	@	91	[	118	v
11	Ctrl-K	38	&	65	A	92	\	119	w
12	Ctrl-L	39	'	66	B	93	]	120	x
13	Return	40	(	67	C	94	^	121	y
14	Ctrl-N	41	)	68	D	95	–	122	z
15	Ctrl-P	42	*	69	E	96	`	123	{
16	Ctrl-Q	43	+	70	F	97	a	124	l
17	Ctrl-R	44	,	71	G	98	b	125	}
18	Ctrl-S	45	–	72	H	99	c	126	~
19	Ctrl-T	46	.	73	I	100	d	127	Delete
20	Ctrl-U	47	/	74	J	101	e		
21	Ctrl-V	48	0	75	K	102	f		
22	Ctrl-W	49	1	76	L	103	g		
23	Ctrl-X	50	2	77	M	104	h		
24	Ctrl-Y	51	3	78	N	105	I		
25	Ctrl-Z	52	4	79	O	106	j		
26	Escape	53	5	80	P	107	k		

that you see on your computer screen are represented inside the computer by numbers. ASCII is a standard way of doing this. For example, in ASCII, 65 means *A*, 66 means *B*, and 67 means *C*. 👁 Look up *ASCII character set*, *computer*, and *screen*.

ASCII character set The *ASCII character set* is a code for letters, numbers, and other symbols. The code is used by computers to represent and to communicate information. 👁 Look up *ASCII* and *code*.

ASCII file An *ASCII file* is a file that contains only ASCII characters.

How are ASCII files different from other files? ASCII files contain only simple text. They are only a sequence of characters. They have no formatting or special codes like, say, word processor files. 👁 Look up *ASCII*, *ASCII character set*, *character*, *file*, *formatting*, and *word processor*.

---

assembly language *Assembly language* is a computer language made of codes that are similar to the actual numerical instructions used by the CPU.

Why do programmers program in assembly language? Programs written in machine language, which assembly language is translated into, can be faster than programs written in a high-level language such as BASIC or C++.

Why do programmers not just program in the language of the CPU instead of assembly language? The language of the CPU is a whole lot of num-

bers. Writing a program in nothing but numbers would be very difficult. The codes of assembly language are more meaningful and easier to work with than numbers. 👁 Look up *BASIC*, *C++*, *code*, *CPU*, *machine language*, and *program*.

---

asterisk (*) An *asterisk* is a star-shaped symbol. Six different styles of asterisks appear below.

(1) In DOS, Windows, OS/2, and UNIX, an asterisk is a wild card. When you want to use a file but are not sure about its file name, you can use an asterisk to replace one or all of the letters in the file name or in the file name extension. For example, *.exe means all the files that end in .exe (the DOS command for finding these files is dir *.exe). 👁 Look up *DOS*, *extension*, *OS/2*, *UNIX*, *wild card*, and *Windows*.

(2) When an asterisk appears next to a word, it means that more facts about that word will be found at the bottom of the page. These additional facts are called footnotes.

---

at sign The symbol @, which stands for *at* is used in e-mail addresses. 👁 Look up *e-mail*.

---

attachment An *attachment* is a file that is sent as part of a piece of e-mail. 👁 Look up *e-mail* and *file*.

---

audible *Audible* means that something can be heard.

audio *Audio* means sound. For example, audio files are sound files. They may be recorded music that you can listen to.

AUP 👁 Look up *acceptable-use policy.*

AUTOEXEC.BAT *AUTOEXEC.BAT* is a file on DOS, Windows 95, and Windows 98 computers that contains instructions that are carried out every time you boot the computer. 👁 Look up *boot, DOS, file,* and *Windows.*

availability The *availability* of a software program is the time when it will be ready for you to buy. 👁 Look up *software program.*

AVI *AVI* stands for **a**udio-**v**ideo **i**nterlace. An AVI file is a format for movie files. When you play an AVI file, you see a movie on your screen. 👁 Look up *file, format,* and *screen.*

.avi The suffix *.avi* means that a file is an AVI movie. 👁 Look up *AVI, file,* and *suffix.*

AYT *AYT* is an abbreviation for "are you there?" It is used in informal e-mail, chat, and Usenet.

Paul: Anybody home? **ayt**

Paul: You must be off-line. I'll try you later.

See the appendix, pages 189–190, for a complete table of abbreviations. 👁 Look up *chat, e-mail,* and *Usenet.*

B The uppercase letter *B* is an abbreviation for byte. 👁 Look up *byte.*

b The lowercase letter *b* is an abbreviation for bit. 👁 Look up *bit.*

<B> tag The *<B> tag* is an HTML tag that makes a word bold on a web page. 👁 Look up *bold, HTML,* and *tag.*

back *Back* is a browser command that will return you to the most recently viewed web page. 👁 Look up *browser* and *web page.*

backbone The *backbone* is the main set of cables or connections in a wide-area network. It carries most of the communication traffic. 👁 Look up *wide-area network.*

Back button The *Back button* is a button on most web browsers that lets you return to a web page that you just viewed. 👁 Look up *browser, Forward button, Home button, Stop button,* and *web page.*

back door Sometimes people access computers, Web sites, or systems in ways they were not meant to. They do this by going through a *back door.* A back door is a way of breaking into a program or web site. Very often, the programmer builds the back door into a program. Sometimes, though, back doors occur unintentionally, by mistake. 👁 Look up *access, program, programmer,* and *web site.*

background The *background* is the color of the screen against which other things are displayed. An example of a noncomputer background is in a school notebook. The background is white, and lines have been displayed on it. 👁 Look up *screen.*

backslash (\ ) The *backslash* is one of the symbols on your keyboard. It is on the same key as the pipe (|), just above the enter key. 👁 Look up *forward slash, keyboard,* and *symbol.*

backspace The *backspace* is one of the keys on your keyboard. The backspace key causes the cursor to move backward. As it moves backward, it erases words one symbol at a time. 👁 Look up *cursor* and *keyboard.*

backup copy When you have an important file, you do not want to risk losing it. A *backup copy* is a copy of a file that you make and store in a safe place. Sometimes people save a backup copy on their hard disk or on a floppy disk different from the one they are using. People also make backup copies when they are making changes to a file and are not sure that they will like the changes. For example, an artist drawing a picture of a clown may save a backup copy, draw a new costume on the clown, and then go back to the backup copy if he or she does not like the new costume.

Should I make backup copies of my files? If they are important to you, then you should make backup copies. If the files are very important to you, then you should store them on a disk and keep the disk in a separate location from your computer. 👁 Look up *file, floppy disk,* and *hard disk.*

backward compatible A new program or a piece of computer hardware is *backward compatible* if it is compatible with earlier versions of the program or hardware. 👁 Look up *hardware, program,* and *version number.*

bad sector The surface of a disk is separated into sectors. Data is stored in these sectors. A *bad sector* is a disk sector that has been damaged in some way and cannot be used to store information. 👁 Look up *data* and *disk.*

BAK *BAK* is an abbreviation for "back at keyboard." It is used in informal e-mail, chat, and Usenet.

> *Anna: Didn't we get a math assignment that's due tomorrow?*
> *Mark: You're right. I forgot all about it. I'd better go get started. I'll talk to you later when I'm **bak**.*

See the appendix, pages 189–190, for a complete table of abbreviations. 👁 Look up *chat, e-mail,* and *Usenet.*

Balloon Help When you read a comic book, you know what is going on by reading the words in the balloons over the characters' heads. On Macintosh computers, if you want help with something on the screen, you can turn on *Balloon Help* and point to the item. A message inside a balloon will then appear to help you. The Balloon Help in the illustration explains the File menu. PC computers have a similar feature, but it is not called Balloon Help because Balloon Help is a trademark of Apple Computers, Incorporated. ◉ Look up *Apple Computers, Incorporated; computer; Macintosh;* and *trademark*.

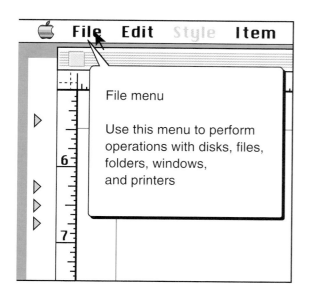

bang *Bang* is the character !, more commonly known as an exclamation mark.

banner A *banner* is a box on a web page that advertises some product or service that someone wants you to buy or use. Banners usually have links that connect you to the advertiser's site when you click them. ◉ Look up *hyperlink* and *web page*.

bar chart A *bar chart* displays information as rectangular figures that represent different values by how high the rectangles rise. Below is an example of a bar chart.

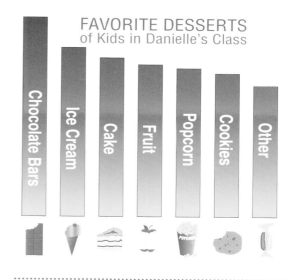

bar code A *bar code* is the code on items sold in stores. It is made up of lines with numbers under each line. A scanner at the register reads the bar code to identify the item. ◉ Look up *scanner*.

bar code reader A *bar code reader* scans the lines on items that you are buying. The information in the bar code, such as price and what the product is, is entered into the

store's computer. Some bar code readers are built into the checkout counter, others are handheld.

baseline The *baseline* is the line at the bottom of a word. The baseline is useful when you are placing text into a document or onto a web page. 👁 Look up *text* and *web page.*

Compute!

BASIC *BASIC* is an acronym for **B**eginners **A**ll-purpose **S**ymbolic **I**nstruction **C**ode. It is a programming language that is very easy to learn and to use. It uses simple codes like PRINT, GOTO, IF, and THEN. To print Hello! on the computer screen, for example, you would simply type the line

PRINT "Hello!"

in a program. BASIC is still used, but most of the programs you will use on your computer are written in more complicated languages like C++ or Java. 👁 Look up *C++, computer, Java, program, programming language,* and *screen.*

baud rate The *baud rate* of a modem is a measure of the speed that the modem can transmit information over transmission lines. The higher the baud rate, the faster the modem sends information. A modem's speed in bits per second is usually twice the baud rate. 👁 Look up *modem.*

bay A *bay* is a space within a computer enclosure that is provided to hold a disk drive or some other device. 👁 Look up *disk drive.*

BBIAF *BBIAF* is an abbreviation for "be back in a few minutes." It is used in informal e-mail, chat, and Usenet.

> Tom: **bbiaf**. *I'll go find the book that you're talking about.*
> Peter: OK.

See the appendix, pages 189–190, for a complete table of abbreviations. 👁 Look up *chat, e-mail,* and *Usenet.*

BBL *BBL* is an abbreviation for "be back later." It is used in informal e-mail, chat, and Usenet.

Jane: Well, I've got to go baby-sit my baby brother. **bbl**. *We can talk more then.*
John: Okay.

See the appendix, pages 189–190, for a complete table of abbreviations. 👁 Look up *chat, e-mail,* and *Usenet.*

BBS *BBS* is an abbreviation for **b**ulletin **b**oard **s**ystem. BBSs were used before the online services became common. A BBS is a computer that allows users to exchange information over phone lines. 👁 Look up *online* and *user.*

beep A *beep* is a sound that computers make that sends a message to the person using the computer. For example, a beep may mean "the key that you pressed will not work at this time" or "your computer is turned on and ready to work."

BEEP *BEEP* is a DOS command that instructs the computer to beep. 👁 Look up *DOS.*

bells and whistles *Bells and whistles* are extra features that may be useful but are probably not absolutely necessary. If you have a pet dog, you could buy it sunglasses, maybe a colorful T-shirt, and a belt. You would then have a dog with all of the bells and whistles! However, your dog would get along fine without these things. Very often computer hardware, computer software, and on-line services come with bells and whistles.

"Juan, do you like the new word processor that your parents bought for your computer?" Robin asked.
"Yes, I like it. It does everything that I want it to, but it has a lot of **bells and whistles** *that I will probably never use," Juan replied.*

Very often bells and whistles can be a serious annoyance. If you have this problem, you can usually turn off the features

of a program that you do not want to use. 👁 Look up *feature, hardware, online, software,* and *word processor.*

---

beta tester A *beta tester* is a person who tests software after it has first been tested at the location of the company that made it.

Can I be a beta tester? Maybe. If you want to be a beta tester, then contact the software companies that make the software you like. They may let you be a beta tester. 👁 Look up *alpha testing, beta test site, beta testing, gamma testing, software,* and *software company.*

---

beta testing When software companies are making new software, they often test the software to be sure that it works properly. Early testing is done at the company. This testing is called alpha testing. Later testing is done outside of the company. This testing is called *beta testing.* Beta testing is named after beta (β), the second letter of the Greek alphabet. Software entering the beta test phase is usually more reliable than software at the alpha test phase. 👁 Look up *alpha testing, beta test site, gamma testing, software,* and *software company.*

---

beta test site A *beta test site* is a place where beta testing of software is done. Computers at beta test sites are widely separated and often do not belong to the company. Beta testing is done just before finish-

ing work on a program, and it is done by beta testers. 👁 Look up *beta tester, program,* and *software.*

....

Big Blue IBM (International Business Machines Corporation) is often called *Big Blue* because blue is the company's color

and because IBM is a major player in the world of computers. 👁 Look up *computer* and *IBM.*

....

<BIG> tag The *<BIG> tag* is an HTML tag that makes text bigger than the other text in a web page. 👁 Look up *HTML, tag, text,* and *web page.*

....

binary numbers The numbers that you use everyday like 9, 37, and 1,479 are called decimal numbers. These numbers are written in base-ten notation, which means that they are made using the symbols 0, 1, 2, 3,

4, 5, 6, 7, 8, and 9. (Notice that there are 10 different symbols!) If you could look inside the microchips of a computer, you would see that computers use numbers like 01, 110, 1100101, and 00111, which use only 1 and 0.

Decimal	Binary	Decimal	Binary
0	0	8	1000
1	1	9	1001
2	10	10	1010
3	11	11	1011
4	100	12	1100
5	101	13	1101
6	110	14	1110
7	111	15	1111

Why do computers use binary numbers in their internal workings instead of decimal numbers? The CPU and memory of a computer are made of a lot of switches (transistors). (In fact, millions and millions of them!) Just like most switches, each of these switches is either

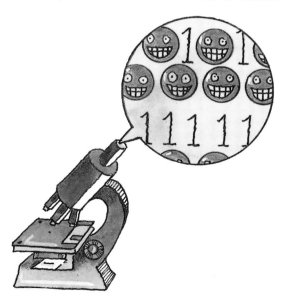

on or off (or 1 for on and 0 for off). So, the easiest way for computers to handle numbers is to use binary numbers because binary numbers use only two symbols, 1 for on and 0 for off. ◉ Look up *CPU, memory,* and *microchip.*

biological feedback device When you use a keyboard or a mouse, it translates your keystrokes and clicks into electric signals to input information. When you use a *biological feedback device,* on the other hand, things like eye movements or movements of your head are tracked and translated into electric signals to input information. Some people are even developing devices that use your brain waves or electric impulses in your nerves to input information. ◉ Look up *device, information, keyboard,* and *mouse.*

bit A *bit* is the smallest piece of information that a computer can store. A bit only has two values, 1 and 0. Bytes are made of 8 bits. Files, like a word processor file, are strings of bytes. ◉ Look up *byte* and *file.*

bitmap A *bitmap* is a sequence of numerical values that store an image. ◉ Look up *image.*

bit-mapped graphics *Bit-mapped graphics* are images represented as a sequence of pixels with no formatting. ◉ Look up *formatting* and *pixels.*

black widow A *black widow* is a destructive program that is downloaded through the World Wide Web as a Java applet. Java language has safeguards to protect against downloaded programs, but a nasty applet can use up memory in your computer and slow it down. ◉ Look up *applet, Java,* and *World Wide Web.*

blink rate The *blink rate* is the number of times the computer's cursor flashes every second. ◉ Look up *computer* and *cursor.*

bloatware Software that uses unreasonable amounts of disk space, memory, or CPU speed is referred to as *bloatware.* ◉ Look up *CPU, disk, memory,* and *software.*

block move A *block move* is the process of moving a section of a file to another place within the same file. Most software programs have an edit function that allows you to block and move text within a file. ◉ Look up *edit, file,* and *software program.*

block protect The *block protect* feature is used to prevent a section of text or a particular chart, table, or other graphic item from being split across pages when printed. 👁 Look up *feature.*

....

blur *Blur* is a paint program feature that gives an image the appearance of being slightly out of focus. 👁 Look up *paint program.*

....

board A *board* is a circuit mounted on a piece of material. A printed circuit board has circuits that connect computer chips mounted on the board. Some boards are small and are installed in expansion slots in your computer to give your computer extra capabilities. The motherboard of a computer contains the CPU and memory chips. 👁 Look up *circuit, CPU, expansion slot, memory,* and *motherboard.*

....

<BODY> The *<BODY>* tag is an HTML tag that indicates the main part of a web page, as distinguished from the head of an HTML document. 👁 Look up *HTML,* tag, and *World Wide Web.*

....

bold Letters or words that are darker than normal are called *bold.*

This is bold.
This is normal type.

....

bold italic Letters or words that are slanted and bold are *bold italic* letters.

This is bold.
This is italic.
This is bold italic.

....

bomb A computer *bombs* when the program that it is running fails. 👁 Look up *computer, crash,* and *program.*

....

bookmark When you are reading a book, you use a *bookmark* to keep your place when you set the book aside for a while. When you are using the Internet, you can bookmark a web page so that you can return to it easily. You usually do this by clicking on a menu item. The name of the page is then added to your list of bookmarked sites. 👁 Look up *click, Internet, menu,* and *web page.*

....

boot To *boot* your computer means to start your computer. Booting is necessary because for a computer to run, certain things must be done. For example, memory must be cleared, and the operating system must be loaded. Booting performs these tasks and many others. The word boot is from the expression "pulling yourself up by your bootstraps." 👁 Look up *cold boot, load, memory, operating system,* and *warm boot.*

boot disk A *boot disk* is a disk or a diskette that you can use to start your computer. 👁 Look up *boot, disk,* and *diskette.*

bootleg (1) To *bootleg* is to copy a program without permission from the owner of the copyright.

(2) A *bootleg* copy is a copy of a program or some other material that has been made without permission from the owner of the copyright. 👁 Look up *copy* and *program.*

bottleneck The part of a computer system that slows down its performance speed is known as a *bottleneck.* It could be a slow disk drive or slow modem, for example. 👁 Look up *disk drive* and *modem.*

bounce Sometimes when you send a message by e-mail, the message will be returned because it cannot reach its destination. When this happens, the message has *bounced.* 👁 Look up *e-mail.*

**
 tag** The *
 tag* is an HTML tag that breaks a line of text. 👁 Look up *HTML, tag,* and *text.*

braces *Braces* are the characters { and }.

brackets *Brackets* are the characters [and].

BRB *BRB* is an abbreviation for "be right back." It is used in informal e-mail, chat, and Usenet.

> *Juan: Oh no! I forgot to feed my dog.*
> **brb**
> *Paul: OK.*

See the appendix, pages 189–190, for a complete table of abbreviations. 👁 Look up *chat, e-mail,* and *Usenet.*

broadband *Broadband* is a way of sending data. By using broadband communication, large amounts of data can be sent very quickly. Broadband is often called high-speed communication. 👁 Look up *data.*

browse To *browse* is to explore the World Wide Web or the contents of a disk or CD-ROM. 👁 Look up *CD-ROM, disk,* and *World Wide Web.*

browser A *browser* is a program that you use to explore the World Wide Web. A browser lets you view the hypertext files of the World Wide Web. These files are packed with information, images, movies, sound files, and programs. The two most popular browsers are Microsoft Internet Explorer and Netscape Navigator. 👁 Look up *file, hypertext, Microsoft Internet Explorer, program,* and *World Wide Web.*

BTDT *BTDT* is an abbreviation for "been there, done that." It is used in informal e-mail, chat, and Usenet.

> *Juan: Have you ever bungee jumped?*
> *Paul: Yep.* **btdt**

See the appendix, pages 189–190, for a complete table of abbreviations. 👁 Look up *chat, e-mail,* and *Usenet.*

BTW *BTW* is an abbreviation for "by the way." It is used in informal e-mail, chat, and Usenet.

> *Juan:* **btw***, is Susan coming to the movie with us?*
> *Jawan: Yes.*

See the appendix, pages 189–190, for a complete table of abbreviations. 👁 Look up *chat, e-mail,* and *Usenet.*

buddy list A *buddy list* is a feature of some online services that lets you know if your friends are logged onto the Internet so that you can communicate with them. To use the feature, you and the other person must be using the same online service. 👁 Look up *feature, Internet, log on, on-line,* and *program.*

bug A *bug* is an error in a computer program. When computer programmers write programs, bugs often occur. These bugs must be corrected if the program is to work. 👁 Look up *program* and *programmer.*

built fraction A *built fraction* is created by setting the numerator and denominator as regular numbers separated by a forward slash (1/3, 1/5). 👁 Look up *case fraction* and *piece fraction.*

bullet A *bullet* is the character •. Bullets are often used to mark items in a list.

bulletin board system (BBS) 👁 Look up *BBS*.

....

burn To *burn* is a slang expression meaning to record information on a CD-ROM. 👁 Look up *CD-ROM* and *information*.

....

burn-in When companies make new computers and peripherals, they often test the equipment by running it before it is shipped. This testing is called *burn-in*. Burning in hardware helps to ensure that it will not fail after the customer buys it. 👁 Look up *computer, hardware,* and *peripherals*.

....

bus A *bus* is a set of wires through which information travels in a computer. An internal bus handles communication from only one part of the computer to another. An external bus interfaces with a computer card that has been inserted into an expansion slot. 👁 Look up *computer* and *expansion slot*.

....

Butterfly key The *Butterfly key* is the ⌘ key on Macintosh computers. It is also called the command key. The Butterfly key is a modifier key. It allows you to change the meaning of other keys by pressing the Butterfly key and the other key at the same

time. 👁 Look up *computer, Macintosh,* and *modifier key*.

....

buzzword A *buzzword* is a technical word or phrase that is currently popular.

....

byte A *byte* is a small piece of information. Bytes are usually made of 8 bits. A bit can stand for only 1 or 0, but a byte can stand for a whole range of values (0–255 for 8-bit bytes, for example). So, bytes can represent letters or numbers. For example, a computer can represent the name *Thomas* using 6 bytes: one byte for *T,* one for *h,* one for *o,* one for *m,* one for *a,* and one for *s.* Also, depending on the type of graphics image, there is roughly one byte for every pixel, or dot, that you see on your screen. 👁 Look up *bit, draw program, graphics, image,* and *pixel*.

....

C++ *C++* is an extremely popular programming language that extended the *C* programming language. Many of the programs that you use are probably programmed in C++. 👁 Look up *program* and *programming language.*

cable A *cable* is a wire that connects computer equipment to other computer equipment or to a cable outlet. 👁 Look up *computer.*

cable modem A *cable modem* is a modem that allows a computer to send and to receive information over cable television lines instead of telephone lines. 👁 Look up *modem.*

cache When you use a web site, many pictures, blocks of text, addresses, and other information are sent to your computer. These files, or short versions of them, are stored in a special place on your disk called a *cache* so that they can be viewed again without having to access the web. By using a cache, repeated access to a site is much faster. For example, when you use a site after the first time, files from the first visit will be in the cache so that your computer will not have to open them again. 👁 Look up *file, hard disk, information, web site,* and *World Wide Web.*

CAD *CAD* is an abbreviation for **C**omputer-**A**ided **D**esign. CAD is the use of a computer and special software to design projects in fields like engineering and architecture. 👁 Look up *software.*

caddy A *caddy* is a holder, often made of plastic, that you put CD-ROMs into to store them. 👁 Look up *CD-ROM* and *CD-ROM drive.*

cancel To *cancel* is to stop your computer from doing something.

Caps Lock key Sometimes you want to type only capital letters. The *Caps Lock key* lets you do this. When you press the Caps Lock key, all of the letters that you type will be capital letters.

card A *card* is a small circuit board. Cards are added to a computer's motherboard to let the computer do extra things. There are

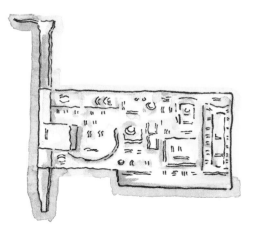

modem cards, sound and graphics cards, and many other kinds of cards.  Look up *graphics, modem,* and *motherboard.*

card slot   A *card slot* is a long, narrow opening on a computer's motherboard. Boards that fit the opening can be put into the computer in a card slot. These boards let the computer do new things or add new data to computer memory.  Look up *computer* and *motherboard.*

carriage return   A *carriage return* moves the cursor to the beginning of the next line. It is called carriage return because old typewriters had a roller, called a carriage, that you had to slide back by using a lever whenever you were at the end of a line. The carriage return key is the same as the Enter key.  Look up *cursor.*

carrier signal   When data is sent, a *carrier signal* is generated and sent over wires (or some other medium). Data is transmitted by changing this signal in ways that modems can recognize and turn back into the original data.  Look up *data* and *modem.*

cartridge font   A *cartridge font* is a container that can be added to a printer. The container holds the design and other facts about a complete set of letters and symbols that you can use to print text.  Look up *printer* and *text.*

case fraction   A *case fraction* is a small fraction that is a single character in a font (½, ¼).  Look up *built fraction* and *piece fraction.*

case insensitive   A program that is *case insensitive* does not notice the difference between uppercase and lowercase. For example, *John* is the same as *john* or even *joHN* for a case-insensitive program.  Look up *case sensitive, lowercase,* and *uppercase.*

case sensitive   Is *Now Showing* the same as *NOW SHOWING*? Although they mean the same thing when we read them, they may mean different things to a computer. If they mean different to the program you are using, then the program is *case sensitive.* The letters *A, B, C,* and so on are uppercase. The letters *a, b, c,* and so on are lowercase. The phrase *Now Showing* is different from *NOW SHOWING* to a case-sensitive program because, to a case-sensitive program, *o* is different from *O, h* is different from *H*, and so on. 👁 Look up *case insensitive* and *program*.

CC (courtesy copy) When you send an e-mail, you may want to send a copy to someone. *CC* is the abbreviation used to describe this copy. 👁 Look up *e-mail*.

CD 👁 Look up *compact disc*.

cd command The MS-DOS and UNIX *cd command* tells your computer to change directories. 👁 Look up *computer, directory, and MS-DOS*, and *UNIX*.

CD-ROM *CD-ROM* is an abbreviation for **c**ompact **d**isk **r**ead-**o**nly **m**emory. A CD-ROM is a CD that has files that your computer can read. The files may be music, games, pictures, utility programs, or even an encyclopedia. A CD-ROM can store much more data than a 3½-inch diskette. A typical CD-ROM can store about 650 megabytes of data. You cannot write data to a CD-ROM without special equipment. 👁 Look up *data, diskette, file, megabyte, memory, ROM*, and *utility program*.

CD-ROM drive 👁 Look up *CD-ROM player*.

CD-ROM player A *CD-ROM player* is what you use to run programs stored on CD-ROM or to play music CDs on your computer. 👁 Look up *CD-ROM*.

Celeron The *Celeron* is a microprocessor that is less expensive than the Pentium II, but has less cache memory. 👁 Look up *cache* and *microprocessor*.

cell A *cell* is a piece of information in a spreadsheet, database, or some other program that organizes information. 👁 Look up *database, information, program,* and *spreadsheet*.

	John	Mary	Tom
Game 1	2345	4245	3325
Game 2	2335	3945	3234
Game 3	3098	3454	3567
TOTAL	7778	11644	10126

cellular modem A *cellular modem* is a modem that uses a cellular telephone to connect to the Internet. 👁 Look up *Internet* and *modem*.

centered text Text that is the same distance from the left as it is from the right side of a page is *centered text*.

> **Some poets use**
> **centered text because they**
> **believe that**
> **different line lengths**
> **make their poetic message stronger.**

centimeter A *centimeter* is a metric unit of length. One inch equals 2.54 centimeters (to the nearest hundredth).

central processing unit  Look up *CPU*.

character A *character* is a letter, number, or symbol that appears on your screen. For example, *A, B, C, 1, 2, 3,* $, %, *, and ? are characters. A character usually requires one byte of storage. Look up *byte*.

character recognition As you read a book, your eyes recognize the characters on the page. The characters make up the words that you read. For example, *cat* is made of the characters *c, a,* and *t.* The abil-ity to recognize characters is called *character recognition*. Some computer devices have character recognition, so they are able to read characters from a page. The data is then input into your computer and used by application programs. Look up *application program, data,* and *device*.

characters per inch Characters are the letters, numbers, and other symbols used in writing. *Characters per inch* tells how many symbols fit into an inch. Look up *program* and *symbol*.

characters per second *Characters per second* is the number of one-byte characters that can be read by a computer in one second. Look up *byte, character,* and *symbol*.

chat *Chat* is a system that lets you talk interactively with other people on the Internet. Look up *Internet*.

chat room A *chat room* is a place on the Internet where you can talk with other people. See the appendix, pages 189–190, for a complete table of abbreviations used in chat. Look up *chat* and *Internet*.

check box A *check box* is a small box on a form that lets you select some feature or option. Look up *feature* and *form*.

chip 👁 Look up *integrated circuit*.

Chooser The *Chooser* is a Macintosh desktop accessory that controls several computer functions. The Chooser displays printer and network icons, for example. 👁 Look up *icon, Macintosh, network,* and *printer*.

chronological order When things are listed in *chronological order,* they are listed in order by date, starting with the first, or oldest, and ending with the last, or newest. They may also be in order, starting with the last, or newest, and ending with the first, or oldest.

1776, 1789, 1812, 1820, 1815

cipher A *cipher* is a system that substitutes one set of letters, numbers, or symbols for another to keep information secret. 👁 Look up *symbol*.

ciphertext *Ciphertext* is a message that has been scrambled so that it cannot be read without the key. Scrambling a message is called encryption. So, ciphertext is an encrypted message. 👁 Look up *encrypt*.

circuit A *circuit* is a set of electronic components on a board wired together so that they do something useful. Circuits are in televisions, VCRs, telephones, radios, CD players, and even coffeemakers. Computers have complicated circuits that let them do all of the things that they do. 👁 Look up *computer*.

circuit board A *circuit board* is a board on which a circuit is mounted. 👁 Look up *circuit*.

Cisco Systems, Inc. This company is the leading provider of high-speed networking hardware. Its web address is *www.cisco.com*.

clean To *clean* is to use an antivirus program to remove viruses from your computer system. 👁 Look up *antivirus program, computer system, infected, program,* and *virus*.

> *"Use the antivirus program to* ***clean*** *that floppy diskette before you use it, son," John's father said.*
> *Later . . .*
> *"I cleaned the diskette, Dad. The antivirus program found one infected file and repaired it."*

click To *click* is to press a button on your mouse, trackball, or other pointing device. 👁 Look up *double-click, mouse,* and *trackball*.

> *John wanted to play his new video game, so he* ***clicked*** *on the game's icon.*

client A *client* is a program or computer served by another program or computer.

Just as a lawyer's client receives the lawyer's services, a client program or computer receives a service from another program or computer. The service it receives is usually data of some sort. A web browser (or the computer running it) is a client, for example. ◉ Look up *browser, data, program,* and *server.*

clip art   *Clip art* is a collection of pictures of many kinds that can be put into a computer's memory and used in drawing pro-

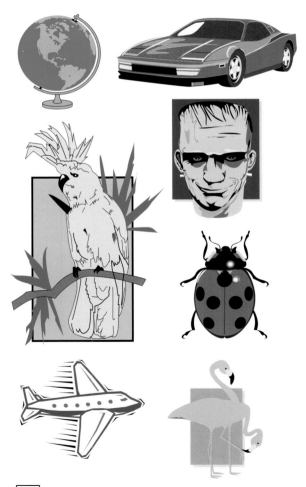

grams to make posters, storybooks, greeting cards, or anything else that you want to illustrate.

*John used his **clip art** file to make 25 different Christmas cards.*

◉ Look up *computer, draw program,* and *memory.*

clock speed   The *clock speed* of a computer tells you how fast the CPU operates. The higher the clock speed, the faster the CPU operates. Clock speed is usually measured in megahertz (MHz). ◉ Look up *computer, CPU,* and *megahertz.*

clockwise   The direction that the hands of a mechanical clock move around the face of the clock is *clockwise.* ◉ Look up *counterclockwise.*

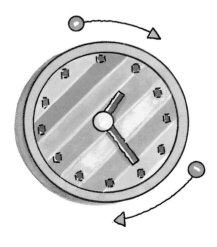

clone   A *clone* is a computer that is a copy of another computer. A clone can do all of the things that the original computer can do. Clones of the IBM PC were widely available long before clones were available for the Macintosh computer, so when people say clone, they usually mean a PC clone. 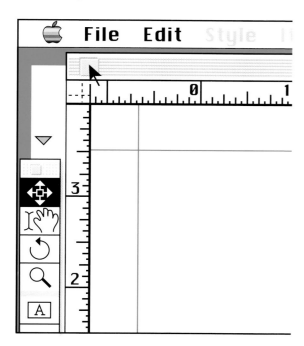 Look up *computer* and *Macintosh*.

close box On Apple computers, the *close box* is the small box in the upper left-hand corner of a window on your screen. This is called the close box because if you click on it, the window will close (or disappear). On PCs using Windows 95 or later versions of

Windows, the box at the top right corner does the same thing. Look up *Apple Computer, Incorporated; PC; window;* and *Windows.*

CLS *CLS* is a DOS command that clears a computer's screen. Look up *DOS.*

cm *cm* is an abbreviation for centimeter. Look up *centimeter.*

code **(1)** When a programmer writes a program, he or she writes lines of instructions that tell the computer to do something. These lines are *code.*

> *"Jane, have you seen this new game? It's radical! Look at all the things you can do," said John.*
> *"Yes, it's great. I read that the program took over a year to write and has over a million lines of* **code***!" Jane said.*

Look up *computer, program,* and *programmer.*

(2) A *code* is a set of specific letters, numbers, or symbols that have a pre-arranged meaning. Look up *symbol.*

codec *Codec* is an abbreviation for **com**pression/**dec**ompression algorithm. Codecs are used to compress and decompress movie files. Look up *algorithm, data compression,* and *decompression.*

Why are movie files compressed and decompressed? Because the files are large, they would be difficult to store and would take a long time to download otherwise. Look up *data compression, decompress,* and *file.*

cold boot To *cold boot* a computer means to boot the computer by turning on the system's power switch when it the computer is off. 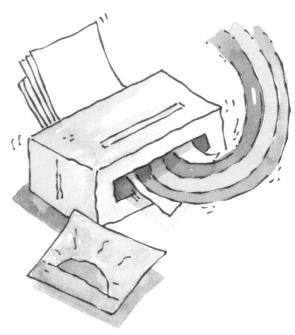 Look up *boot, computer, cold start,* and *warm boot.*

    Warning: If you turn a computer off, waiting a little while before you turn it on is usually better. Read your owner's manual to find out about the proper waiting time.

cold start Look up *cold boot.*

color printer A *color printer* is a printer that can reproduce colors as well as black and white. A color printer could be used to print a

rainbow or a fire engine with all of their colors. Color printers use basic colors (red, blue, and green) to reproduce all other colors.

"Wow," Jane said. "Look at the fantastic sunset that the color printer printed!"

column When information is arranged so that each piece of information is placed on top of the next, this vertical stack is called a *column.* Usually, the information is read from top to bottom.

C	A	1	6A
O	B	2	6B
L	C	3	6C
U	D	4	6D
M	F	5	6E
N	F	6	6F

*Ms. Jones created a spreadsheet for her art class. The spreadsheet had **columns** for test scores, quizzes, and homework scores.*

Look up *information.*

com *com* is a top-level Internet domain name that indicates a corporation or a business. Look up *edu, gov, net,* and *org.*

command A *command* is an order to a computer to do a specific thing. Commands can be given by keystrokes or by using a mouse. Look up *keystroke* and *mouse.*

command key The *command key* is the ⌘ key on Macintosh keyboards.

The command key is also called the Butterfly key. It is a modifier key. Modifier keys change the meaning of other keys. 👁 Look up *keyboard, Macintosh,* and *modifier key.*

communicate To *communicate* is to exchange information. There are many ways to communicate. When you talk, you are communicating. When you write a letter and send it to someone, you are communicating. Computers and computer networks have become excellent tools for communicating.

In addition, pieces of equipment can communicate with each other. For example, your computer communicates with its printer. 👁 Look up *information,* and *network.*

communications software *Communications software* is a program that allows a computer to communicate with other computers over telephone lines or some other medium. 👁 Look up *computer, modem, program,* and *software.*

compact disc (CD) A *compact disc* is a shiny plastic disc on which music or data can be stored. A CD-ROM is a compact disc used to store programs or data. Many software programs now come on compact discs. 👁 Look up *data, program,* and *software program.*

compact disc, read-only memory 👁 Look up *CD-ROM.*

Compaq *Compaq* was the first company to manufacture a PC clone—the first PC-compatible computer that was not made by IBM. Its web address is *http://www.Compaq.com.* 👁 Look up *clone, IBM,* and *PC.*

compatible Two things are *compatible* if they get along and can work together. If you have pets and they get along and play together, then you could say that they are compatible. However, if they do not get along, then they are not compatible. Some

computer equipment is compatible and some is not. For example, a printer made to be used with a PC computer is compatible with PC computers. On the other hand, a Macintosh mouse is not compatible with a PC computer. 👁 Look up *Macintosh, mouse, PC,* and *printer.*

component A *component* is part of a larger device or program. For example, the dictionary program that comes with a word-processing program is a component of the word-processing program. 👁 Look up *device, program,* and *word processor.*

compress 👁 Look up *data compression.*

compression 👁 Look up *data compression.*

CompuServe *CompuServe* is an online information service that can be accessed by modem. Since 1998, it has been a subsidiary of AOL. 👁 Look up *AOL* and *modem.*

computer (1) A *computer* is a machine that can follow a list of instructions of things to do. Automobiles, bicycles, or even blenders are machines, but they are not computers. Even though they do things,

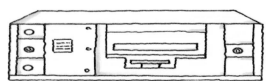

they cannot follow a list of instructions. Only a computer can do that.

Are clocks computers? Simple clocks that only tell the time are not computers. On the other hand, if a clock can be programmed, then it contains a computer.

Are humans computers? Most people would say that humans are not computers, even though humans can follow instructions to do things. Humans can do many things that computers cannot do, at least not yet.

(2) When you are talking about a computer system, especially a PC computer system, the rectangular box in which the motherboard is located is called the *computer.*

(3) A *computer* is a complete computer setup, including keyboard, hard disk drive, monitor, pointing device, and usually peripherals such as a printer and scanner. 👁 Look up *computer system, hard drive, keyboard, monitor, motherboard, peripheral, pointing device, printer, program,* and *scanner.*

computer camp A *computer camp* is a place where people go to learn about computers and the Internet.

> *John went to **computer camp** last summer. He learned C++ programming and web design.*

👁 Look up *computer* and *Internet*.

computer center (1) A *computer center* is a room where computers are available for people to use. For example, many schools and libraries have computer centers.

(2) A *computer center* is a room or group of rooms where computer equipment is stored. 👁 Look up *computer.*

computer game A *computer game* is a program that lets you play some kind of game on your computer. Some games can be played against the computer, while others allow you to play against a human opponent.

> *John said, "I love this game. I am already on level four. On level five, I have to slay the dragon to save the princess."*

👁 Look up *program.*

computer jargon The words or groups of words that have a special meaning when used to talk about computers are *computer jargon.* For example, to *boot* a computer means to start it. A person who does not know computer jargon may think that *boot*

the computer means to kick it! 👁 Look up *boot* and *computer.*

computer laboratory A *computer laboratory* is a room where computers are available for people to use. Many schools have computer laboratories.

computer language 👁 Look up *programming language.*

computer literate If you can understand something about computers and can use computers fairly well to do things, then you are *computer literate.*

computer program A *computer program* is what you use when you play a computer game, use a word processor, send e-mail, or do anything else on a computer. A program is a list of instructions that the computer follows. People usually just say *program* instead of *computer program*.  Look up *e-mail* and *word processor*.

computer science *Computer science* is the study of computers and everything having to do with computers.

computer screen A *computer screen* is the glass surface on the front of the monitor. Information that is computed or retrieved is seen on the computer screen. Look up *information* and *monitor*.

computer store A *computer store* is a store that sells computers, software, computer peripherals, and accessories.

Look up *computer, peripheral,* and *software*.

computer system A *computer system* is a complete computer setup, including keyboard, hard disk drive, monitor, pointing device, and usually peripherals such as a printer and scanner. A computer system is often simply called a computer. Look up *hard drive, keyboard, monitor, peripheral, printer,* and *scanner*.

computer user A *computer user* is a person who uses a computer. When you use your computer to play computer games, to draw a picture, to write e-mail to your friends, or to do anything else with it, you are a computer user. Look up *computer* and *e-mail*.

computer user group A *computer user group* is a group of people who meet to discuss computers. Look up *computer*.

computer virus Look up *virus*.

conferencing *Conferencing* takes place through the use of computer networks. It allows workers to communicate without time differences while working together. Look up *IRC*.

CONFIG.SYS *CONFIG.SYS* is a file used by the DOS and the OS/2 operating systems. The CONFIG.SYS file contains system information and is read when your computer boots. Look up *boot, computer, DOS, file, information, operating system,* and *OS/2*.

configure When you *configure* a computer or program it means that you set it up to be used in a particular way. Some software packages have to be configured. They have to be set up for a certain computer or for a specific user's preferences. 👁 Look up *program* and *software.*

connect To *connect* means to link computers together somehow so that they can exchange information. 👁 Look up *computer* and *information.*

connect time *Connect time* is the amount of time that your computer is connected to the Internet. Most people use the Internet by connecting to an Internet service provider. Often, there is a charge based on connect time. 👁 Look up *connect, Internet,* and *Internet service provider.*

content provider A *content provider* is a company or organization that provides information online. The National Broadcasting Company (NBC) is a content provider for world news at *www.ms.nbc.com.* 👁 Look up *information* and *online.*

context-sensitive help A Help feature that gives you information about what you are doing at the time is called *context-sensitive help.* For example, if you are writing a letter, context-sensitive help will give you information about writing a letter. This may include, for instance, the formats of different kinds of letters and advice about choosing fonts. In many windows programs, context-sensitive menus appear when you click the right mouse button. 👁 Look up *feature, information,* and *program.*

continuous paper *Continuous paper* is paper that comes in long rolls or in large stocks made of hundreds of pages. The paper is fed through a printer using a tractor feed (toothed wheels that fit into holes on the sides of the paper). Some continuous paper has perforations between the pages to use when separating the pages.

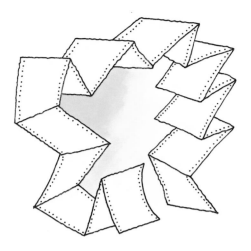

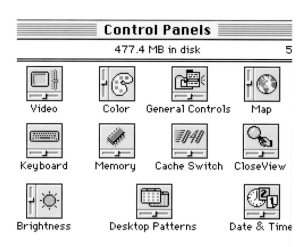

👁 Look up *perforations, printer,* and *tractor feed.*

control key The *control key* is a modifier key on PC and Macintosh keyboards. It is pressed at the same time that another key is pressed to give the second key a different meaning. 👁 Look up *keyboard, Macintosh, modifier key,* and *PC.*

control panel The *control panel* is a folder with utility programs that let you choose how your computer works. For example, settings for your modem are kept in a file in

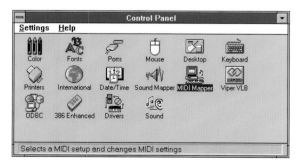

the control panel. You can find the control panel in the Start menu of PC computers or in the Apple menu of Macintosh computers. 👁 Look up *Apple menu, file, folder, Macintosh, modem,* and *utility program.*

cookie Normal cookies, like chocolate chip cookies, are what you have for dessert. In computer terminology, on the other hand, *cookies* are data sent to your computer and copied onto your hard disk when you use the World Wide Web to look at web pages. Cookies allow a web site to keep track of who has visited the site. Concerns have been raised in some quarters about privacy issues involved with leaving cookies behind. 👁 Look up *data, hard drive, web page,* and *World Wide Web.*

copy To *copy* a file means to make a duplicate of the file and store the duplicate in another location, such as on a disk or in memory. 👁 Look up *disk, file,* and *memory.*

COPY command The *COPY command* is a DOS and OS/2 command that makes a copy of a file. 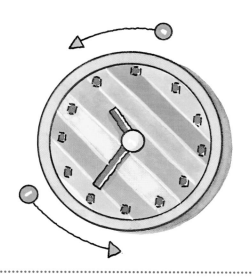 Look up *command, DOS, file,* and *OS/2.*

copy protected A file is *copy protected* if it cannot be duplicated.

corrupt file A *corrupt file* is a file that has been damaged in some way. The damage may have been caused by the software you were using, by a disk controller error, or by the neighbor's kid using the diskette as a target for his new water gun. Look up *file* and *software.*

counterclockwise The direction that the hands of a mechanical clock move around the face of a clock is called clockwise. *Counterclockwise* is the opposite direction. Look up *clockwise.*

courtesy copy Look up *CC.*

cp *cp* is a UNIX command that instructs the computer to copy a file. Look up *command, file,* and *UNIX.*

cpi *cpi* is an abbreviation for **c**haracters **p**er **i**nch. Look up *characters per inch.*

cps *cps* is an abbreviation for **c**haracters **p**er **s**econd. Look up *characters per second.*

CPU *CPU* is an acronym for **c**entral **pro**cessing **u**nit. The CPU decodes and executes program instructions. Look up *program.*

cracker A person who breaks into computers through the Internet and uses them without permission is a *cracker.* Look up *hacker.*

crash A *crash* happens when a computer stops working because its hardware or software fails. Crashes are not usually the fault of the computer user. Software bugs can cause crashes. Sometimes, recovering from a crash is possible, but you must often restart your computer if it crashes.

"Johnny, why are there no illustrations in your report?" Johnny's teacher asked.

"I had a computer problem. Every time I tried to print the illustrations, my computer crashed." Johnny said.

Look up *bug, computer user, hardware,* and *software.*

creeping featurism *Creeping featurism* is the result of adding features to software in an unorganized way. It results in a product that is difficult to use and less reliable. Look up *bells and whistles* and *software.*

CRT *CRT* is an abbreviation for **c**athode **r**ay **t**ube. Televisions and standard computer monitors are cathode ray tubes. Look up *monitor.*

Ctrl key Look up *control key.*

Ctrl-Alt-Del On IBM PC computers, *Ctrl-Alt-Del* is a key combination that warm boots the computer. Look up *boot, PC,* and *warm boot.*

cue A *cue* is a prompt that is placed in a program to let the user know something is about to happen. Look up *program* and *prompt.*

CUL8R *CUL8R* is an abbreviation for "see you later." It is used in informal e-mail, chat, and Usenet.

> *Juan: I've got to go eat dinner. My mom's calling me.*
> *Jane: OK, **cul8r**.*

See the appendix, pages 189–190, for a complete table of abbreviations. Look up *chat, e-mail,* and *Usenet.*

current directory The directory used to store or find information for the program in use is called the *current directory.* Look up *directory, information,* and *program.*

current drive The *current drive* is the drive that your computer uses unless you instruct it to use another drive.

cursor The *cursor* is a symbol that helps you to keep your place on the computer screen, just as you may use your finger to keep your place in a book. It may be a solid rectangle, a blinking rectangle, a vertical line, a horizontal line, or any of a few other symbols.

Computer screens can be full of information. You need the cursor to help you find your way around all that information. When you are typing, the letters and numbers that you type appear at the cursor.

Is the pointer a cursor? Yes, the pointer is a kind of cursor. 👁 Look up *screen* and *symbol*.

cursor movement keys *Cursor movement keys* are keys with arrows on them that move the cursor in one of four directions.

cut To *cut* is to remove material from a document you are editing and store it in a holding area for later use. 👁 Look up *copy* and *paste*.

CYA *CYA* is an abbreviation for "see ya." It is used in informal e-mail, chat, and Usenet.

> *Darius: I have soccer practice, **cya**.*
> *Paul: **cya**.*

See the appendix, pages 189–190, for a complete table of abbreviations. 👁 Look up *chat, e-mail,* and *Usenet.*

cyberspace *Cyberspace* is the world of the Internet, the World Wide Web, and any other computer system that humans can use.

> *"Johnny, why don't you go to the movies with us on Saturday?" Jane asked.*
> *"Thanks, but my new computer just got in. I can't wait to get into cyberspace," Johnny said.*

👁 Look up *Internet* and *World Wide Web.*

cybersurfing 👁 Look up *surf the net.*

daemon A *daemon* is a program that runs continuously to do some particular thing. For example, if your computer alerts you when you have e-mail, then a daemon is probably monitoring your e-mail and giving you a message when new mail arrives. ◉ Look up *e-mail* and *program*.

dagger A *dagger* is the character †.

daisy chain A *daisy chain* is a set of several computer devices connected together,

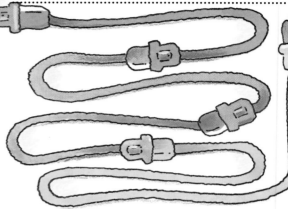

Always turn off your computer and unplug it before connecting or unhooking any computer equipment.

each to the next in the chain. ◉ Look up *computer* and *device*.

dash A *dash* (—) is a punctuation mark. The dash is often typed as two hyphens (--).

data *Data* are pieces of information. Almost everything that computers and the Internet do concerns data. When you play a video game, the images of dragons or knights are stored in the computer as data. When you download a file from the Internet, you are downloading data. ◉ Look up *download, file, image,* and *Internet*.

database Information stored in a computer so that it can be located and shown on the screen is a *database*. A database holds information about a specific topic and maintains relationships between various data elements.  Look up *information* and *screen*.

database administrator A *database administrator* is a person who manages the information that goes into a database. Look up *database* and *information*.

data center A *data center* is a place where computers and computer equipment are kept.

data compression Data files can be large, but they can usually be packed down into a smaller size, just like when you pack a lot of things into your suitcase. *Data compression* lets you fit more data onto your disks and transmit data faster over the Internet. Look up *data, disk, file,* and *Internet.*

data entry When you enter information into a computer, you are doing *data entry.* The data can be typed in by a person or entered by a machine. For example, a company may keep a mailing list of its customers in a database. Data entry would be the job of inputting customers' names, addresses, and other information into the database. Look up *computer* and *database.*

data field A *data field* is a place where you input specific information. Databases, spreadsheets, electronic forms, and other programs have data fields. For example, if you use a Web site, you may have to fill out

an electronic form. The form might ask for your name and address. If so, there will be data fields for you to enter this information. 👁 Look up *database, field, form, information, program, spreadsheet,* and *web site.*

data file The information that you enter and the work that you do when you use a program is stored in a *data file*. Data files can be stored on a disk. 👁 Look up *data, disk, information,* and *program.*

data processing *Data processing* is any computer activity that manages information. 👁 Look up *data.*

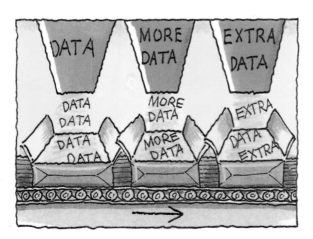

data transfer rate The *data transfer rate* is the speed at which information moves, in units per second, from one computer device to another. The data transfer rate is usually expressed in bits per second. 👁 Look up *bit, device,* and *information.*

date The *date* is the day, month, and year, which most computers keep track of. Files can be listed and retrieved by date.

DATE command You can see and/or change the date by using the *DATE command* in DOS systems. 👁 Look up *command* and *DOS.*

daughterboard A *daughterboard* is a small circuit board that plugs into a larger circuit board. 👁 Look up *circuit board* and *motherboard.*

DBA *DBA* is an abbreviation for **d**ata**b**ase **a**dministrator. 👁 Look up *database administrator.*

debug Computer programs are often large and complex. When computer programmers write programs, very often some unintentional mistakes occur. Programmers

call these mistakes bugs. To *debug* a program means to find and to correct the bugs. 👁 Look up *bug, program,* and *programmer.*

....

decimal *Decimal* numbers are the numbers that we use every day. Decimal numbers are also called base-ten numbers. 👁 Look up *binary numbers* and *hexadecimal.*

....

decompress Often, computer files are compressed, which means that they have been packed into a smaller size. This is especially true of images and video files. To *decompress* a file is to expand information back to its original form. 👁 Look up *data compression, file, image,* and *information.*

....

decrypt To *decrypt* is to change information from scrambled code into its original form. To do this, the user needs a password and the key to the code. Modern encryption methods use mathematical techniques to make codes that are very difficult, or impossible, to break without the password and key. 👁 Look up *encrypt, information,* and *password.*

....

dedicated If something is *dedicated* it means that it is restricted to serving only one function, such as a telephone line that is only used for a fax machine.

....

default A *default* is something that the computer will do unless the user instructs the computer to do something else. For example, a computer will print documents on the default printer unless it is instructed to use some other printer. The user can usually change default settings. 👁 Look up *computer* and *printer.*

....

defragment Sometimes data on a disk is scattered and disorganized. To *defragment* a disk is to run a disk defragmenter that arranges the data on the disk in a way that uses disk space more efficiently. This allows your computer to retrieve files faster. 👁 Look up *access, data, disk,* and *file.*

....

DEL command To remove one or more files from your MS-DOS computer, use the *DEL command.* 👁 Look up *command* and *file.*

....

delete key The *delete key* is a key located on the upper right-hand side of most keyboards. The delete key is used to erase characters when you make a mistake. 👁 Look up *character* and *keyboard.*

....

demagnetize Diskettes store information magnetically. If a disk is placed near a magnet, the magnet may change the magnetic patterns on the disk and ruin the data on the disk. When this happens, the disk has been *demagnetized*. 👁 Look up *data* and *information*.

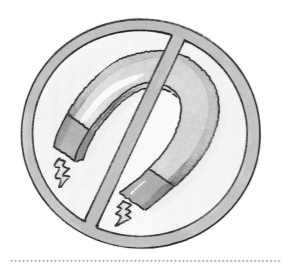

---

demon 👁 Look up *daemon*.

---

density How tightly information is stored on a disk is the *density* of the disk.

The higher the density of a storage device, the more information that it can hold. 👁 Look up *device, disk,* and *information*.

---

descender The part of a letter that falls below the baseline of a word is called a *descender*. The baseline is an imaginary line at the bottom of words. Five letters have descenders: *g, j, p, q,* and *y*. 👁 Look up *ascender* and *baseline*.

Baby Buggy Bumpers

---

descending order To put things into *descending order* is to start with the greatest value in a list first, the second greatest next, and so on until the smallest value is listed last. For example, the numbers 1 through 10 in descending order are 10, 9, 8, 7, 6, 5, 4, 3, 2, 1. 👁 Look up *text*.

....

desktop (1) The *desktop* is the first screen that you see on your computer's monitor after your computer has been started. It displays the icons that represent files and programs in your computer. The user can add icons to or delete icons from the desktop.

(2) *Desktop* means desktop computer. 👁 Look up *computer, desktop computer, file, icon, monitor,* and *screen*.

....

desktop computer A *desktop computer* is a computer designed to fit on an office desk or on a table and is generally not portable. Laptop computers are designed to fit on your lap and other computers are designed to sit on the floor. 👁 Look up *laptop computer*.

....

desktop publishing (DTP) When you use your personal computer, word processor, and a high-resolution printer to make Christmas cards, invitations, fliers, or books, you are doing *desktop publishing*.  Look up *computer* and *printer*.

destination disk 👁 Look up *target disk*.

device A *device* is any electronic or mechanical thing that does something.

device driver A *device driver* is a utility program that your computer uses to run a device such as a floppy drive, a hard drive, a printer, or a modem. 👁 Look up *hard*

drive, modem, printer, program, and *utility program*.

DHTML *DHTML* is an acronym for **D**ynamic **H**yper**t**ext **M**arkup **L**anguage. DHTML is an improvement on HTML that allows greater user interaction and a wider range of displays. 👁 Look up *HTML*.

dial-up connection The connection between computers created by dialing a telephone number through a modem is a *dial-up connection*. 👁 Look up *modem*.

dialog box A *dialog box* is a request by a program for information from the user. The request appears in a box on your screen. 👁 Look up *information* and *user*.

digital A device is *digital* when it operates by electric on and off states. For example, computers are digital devices. 👁 Look up *device*.

digital photography *Digital photography* is photography that can be processed into images that can be viewed and edited directly on a computer. Instead of using film to capture an image, a digital camera uses a device that records the image as an array of pixels. 👁 Look up *device, image,* and *pixel.*

DIIK *DIIK* is an abbreviation for "darned if I know." It is used in informal e-mail, chat, and Usenet.

Darius: What happens if we miss three practices?
Juan: diik, but it can't be good!

See the appendix, pages 189–190, for a complete table of abbreviations. 👁 Look up *chat, e-mail,* and *Usenet.*

DIKU *DIKU* is an abbreviation for "do I know you?" It is used in informal e-mail, chat, and Usenet.

John: You seem familiar. diku
Paul: I think we may have been in the same chat room a few days ago.

See the appendix, pages 189–190, for a complete table of abbreviations. 👁 Look up *chat, e-mail,* and *Usenet.*

dimmed A menu option that shows up in light gray rather than black type is *dimmed* and is not available for selection. If you click on a dimmed command, nothing will happen. For example, if you want to copy text, the copy command will remain dimmed until you block the text you want to copy.

dingbats *Dingbats,* such as ☆ ✿ ✸ ❖ ☙, are characters that are neither numbers nor mathematical symbols.

DIR command The *DIR command* is a DOS command that tells your computer to show all the files in the directory you are using. 👁 Look up *computer, directory, DOS,* and *file.*

directory A *directory* is a file that organizes other files. A directory usually has parent directories and subdirectories. For example, your hard disk's directory may have subdirectories for DOS and for

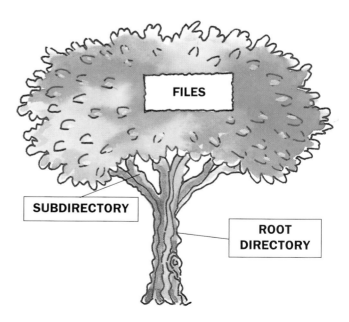

FILES

SUBDIRECTORY

ROOT DIRECTORY

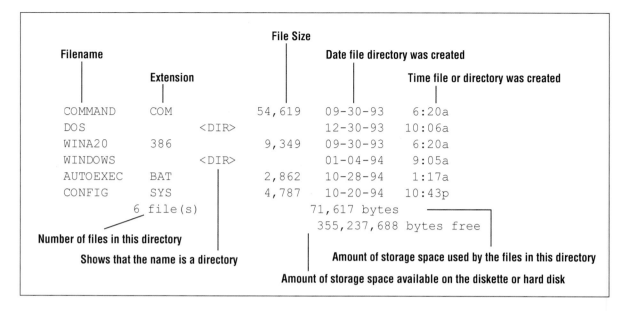

Filename

Extension

File Size

Date file directory was created

Time file or directory was created

```
COMMAND    COM            54,619    09-30-93    6:20a
DOS                <DIR>            12-30-93   10:06a
WINA20     386             9,349    09-30-93    6:20a
WINDOWS            <DIR>            01-04-94    9:05a
AUTOEXEC   BAT             2,862    10-28-94    1:17a
CONFIG     SYS             4,787    10-20-94   10:43p
         6 file(s)                 71,617 bytes
                           355,237,688 bytes free
```

Number of files in this directory

Shows that the name is a directory

Amount of storage space used by the files in this directory

Amount of storage space available on the diskette or hard disk

applications such as games. 👁 Look up *directory, DOS, file,* and *hard drive.*

....

directory tree A *directory tree* is a list of directories and subdirectories organized in a tree, starting with the root (or base) directory. 👁 Look up *directory.*

....

disable To *disable* a device, a program, or a feature of a program is to turn it off. For example, you can disable Java on a Web browser. To do this, set your security feature so that it is impossible for Java programs to be downloaded and run on your computer. Another example is that when you use a word processor, you can disable automatic spell checking and your computer will not check your spelling as you type. 👁 Look up *browser, Java, program, word processor,* and *World Wide Web.*

....

disc *Disc* (with a *c*) means a compact disc (a CD or a CD-ROM). 👁 Look up *CD-ROM.*

....

disk *Disk* (with a *k*) means a diskette, Zip disk, or hard disk. 👁 Look up *diskette, hard drive,* and *ZIP disk.*

....

disk defragmenter A *disk defragmenter* is a program that arranges data on a disk in a manner that uses disk space more efficiently. This allows your computer to access files faster. 👁 Look up *access, data, disk, file,* and *program.*

....

disk drive A *disk drive* is a device that allows your computer to read data and to write data to a disk. Hard disks, diskette drives, and CD-ROM drives are all disk drives. 👁 Look up *CD-ROM* *player, data, device, diskette drive,* and *hard drive.*

Disk First Aid *Disk First Aid* will examine your diskette and repair problems automatically. Disk First Aid is a Macintosh program. 👁 Look up *diskette* and *program.*

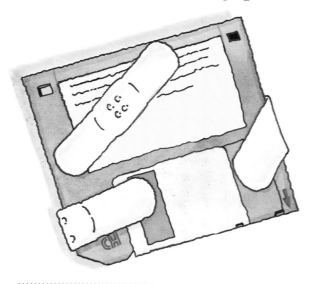

disk jacket A *disk jacket* is a cover that protects 5¼-inch diskettes from dust or scratches. 5¼-inch diskettes are almost obsolete. The 3½-inch high-density disk is currently the most popular diskette. 👁 Look up *diskette.*

disk shutter The sliding metal bar on a 3½-inch diskette is the *disk shutter.* The magnetic disk inside a 3½-inch diskette stores information. The disk shutter protects the disk from dust or scratches. 👁 Look up *diskette* and *information.*

disk sleeve 👁 Look up *disk jacket.*

DISKCOPY command The *DISKCOPY command* is used to copy all the information on a diskette to another diskette. The DISKCOPY command is a DOS command. 👁 Look up *diskette* and *information.*

diskette A *diskette* is a small, removable disk that your computer can store data on. Both the 5¼-inch and the 3½-inch disks are called diskettes. The most popular diskette is the 3½-inch diskette. 👁 Look up *diskette* and *floppy disk.*

diskette drive The *diskette drive* is a device that allows a user to read and write data to a floppy disk. 👁 Look up *data, device,* and *user.*

docking station A device that you can attach a laptop computer to is a *docking station.* A docking station may contain a charger and/or equipment to give the laptop extra features, such as a larger monitor.  👁 Look up *feature*.

document (1) A *document* is a file written and saved on a PC computer.

   (2) To *document* is to write and save an explanation of something. 👁 Look up *file, PC,* and *save*.

documentation When you buy a program or computer equipment, you need instructions and other information about your purchase so that you can use it properly. These instructions and information are *documentation*. Documentation is usually included with programs or computer equipment when you buy them, and additional documentation may be available on-line. If you download a program, make sure that you also download any documentation that you may need to use the program or to register your ownership with the selling company. 👁 Look up *download, online,* and *program*.

domain address A *domain address* is an Internet address that is in a readable form, such as *Smith.com,* as distinguished from an IP address, which consists of numbers. 👁 Look up *IP address*.

DOS *DOS* is an acronym for **d**isk **o**perating **s**ystem. An operating system is a program that manages the computer. DOS is usually short for MS-DOS, which was the standard system for IBM PCs. The DOS system is not powerful enough for today's PCs and is quickly being replaced by Windows. 👁 Look up *acronym, program,* and *Windows*.

DOS command The *DOS command* allows you to communicate with a DOS-based computer. The DOS command is entered by typing it at the DOS prompt. 👁 Look up *communicate* and *computer*.

DOSKEY The *DOSKEY* allows the user to store commands so that they will be executed in the same order each time the DOSKEY is entered. This feature is available in MS-DOS 5.0 and later. 👁 Look up *command* and *user.*

DOS prompt The *DOS prompt* is a message on your screen that tells you that the computer has executed one DOS command and another command can be entered. 👁 Look up *command* and *screen*.

---

dot com *Dot com* is the Internet domain suffix .com. The suffix .com indicates that a Web page is for a corporation or business. 👁 Look up *net* and *org*.

---

dot-matrix printer A *dot-matrix printer* is a printer that uses an array of dots pressed onto paper to form patterns of letters, numbers, symbols, and images. 👁 Look up *image, printer,* and *symbol.*

---

dot pitch The *dot pitch* is the smallest dot that your computer monitor can display. Many small dots make a better picture than do a few large dots. 👁 Look up *monitor.*

---

dots per inch Computer monitors and printers make images by using dots. *Dots per inch* is a measure of the number of dots that a monitor or printer can make in one inch. The greater the number of dots per inch, the higher the quality of the image. In an image, dots are so close together that they look solid. For example, this is how a printer writes DATA:

This is how the word looks when so many dots are used that you cannot see the space between them:

For many years, astronomers believed the lines that they saw on the surface of Mars were large ditches called canals.

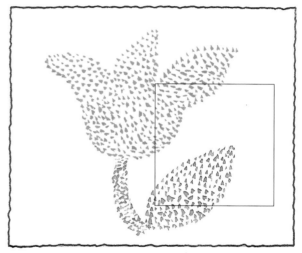

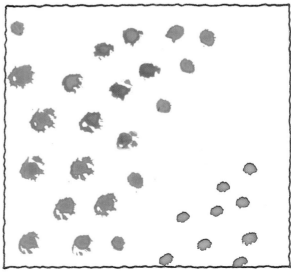

When the first close-up satellite pictures were received, the canals turned out to be lines of dots made by meteor holes on the surface of the planet. The reason why the holes looked solid is that, even with telescopes, the spaces between the holes were too small to see from Earth. 👁 Look up *printer* and *symbol*.

double-click To *double-click* means to click a mouse button twice rapidly in succession.

`PC` On PC computers, you double-click by clicking the button on the left.

`Mac` On Macintosh computers, you double-click by clicking the single mouse button.

When do I double-click and when do I just click once? Clicking and double-clicking usually mean different things. You usually click when you want to choose something. You double-click if you want to choose something and to have what you choose do something more. For example, in Windows, clicking on a file name will display the file, while double-clicking on a file name lets you see and change the file name, delete the file, and so on. 👁 Look up *file, Macintosh, mouse, PC,* and *Windows*.

double-density Single-density disks were the first floppy disks. They could hold 360 kilobytes of information. *Double-density* disks were developed later. Double-density, double-sided 3½-inch diskettes could store 720 kilobytes of information. The 3½-inch single- and 3½-inch double-density diskettes are no longer used. The 3½-inch high-density diskettes, which store 1.44 megabytes

of information, have taken their place. 👁 Look up *floppy disk, information,* and *kilobyte*.

down When a computer has stopped working, it has gone *down*. A computer can be down because of a malfunction or because of maintenance or upgrade. 👁 Look up *computer* and *malfunction*.

down arrow key The *down arrow key* is the ⬇ key on your keyboard. The down arrow key moves the cursor down one line each time the key is pressed. 👁 Look up *cursor*.

download When you *download* a file from another computer, the file is sent to you, usually over telephone lines using your computer's modem. 👁 Look up *file, FTP, modem,* and *upload*.

downtime (1) *Downtime* is the amount of time that a computer is broken.

(2) *Downtime* is the amount of time that a working computer is not being used.

dpi *dpi* is an abbreviation for **d**ots **p**er **i**nch. dpi is used to describe the quality of a printer. The higher the dpi, the higher the quality. 👁 Look up *printer*.

draft quality *Draft quality* is a measure of how a print looks. Draft quality looks good enough to make sure that the right information is on the page but does not look good enough to use for letters or other documents. Draft quality was found on older dot-matrix printers. The draft-quality setting was useful because it was much faster than letter quality. 👁 Look up *dot-matrix printer, information,* and *printer.*

drag To *drag* means to hold down the mouse button to move something on your computer screen.

Mac To drag an object on a Macintosh computer, you hold down the only mouse button.
PC To drag an object on PC computers, you hold down the left mouse button.

What is dragging used for? Dragging has many uses. On Macintosh computers, for example, you can drag the icon of a CD or floppy disk into the trash can to eject the

CD or disk. On PC or Macintosh computers, you can drag the corner of a window to change the size of the window. In draw programs, you can use dragging to move an object to a different part of a picture. 👁 Look up *compact disc, draw program, floppy disk, icon, Macintosh, mouse button, PC,* and *window.*

draw program A *draw program* is a graphics program that lets you create images, store them, and use them in applications.

How is a draw program different from a paint program? The major difference between draw programs and paint programs is that draw programs treat an image as a collection of objects, while paint programs treat an image as an array of pixels. A draw program allows you to change images by manipulating their individual parts. For example, if you are working with an image of a building on a draw program, you could draw a window and then move the entire window to a new location by clicking on it and dragging it to the new

location. Selecting just the window would be harder in a paint program. 👁 Look up *drag, image, paint program,* and *pixel.*

drive *Drive* is short for disk drive. 👁 Look up *disk drive.*

drive bay The space in the computer enclosure that can hold a disk drive is known as the *drive bay.* 👁 Look up *disk drive.*

drop-down menu 👁 Look up *pull-down menu.*

drop shadow A *drop shadow* is a dark area attached to and offset from an image that makes edges visible. The effect is usually to make the image look three-dimensional. 👁 Look up *image.*

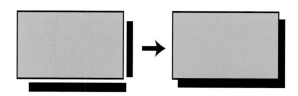

DSL *DSL* is an abbreviation for **d**igital **s**ub-scriber **l**ine. DSL gives you high-speed access to the Internet. DSL can deliver data at 1,500,000 bits per second, while older phone lines could deliver no more than 56,000 bits per second. Because of the larg-er capacity, DSL can compete with cable delivery and fiber optics. 👁 Look up *56k modem, bit, data, digital, fiber optics, Internet, modem,* and *twisted pair.*

DTP *DTP* is an abbreviation for **d**esk**t**op publishing. 👁 Look up *desktop publishing.*

DTS DTS is an abbreviation for "don't think so." It is used in informal e-mail, chat, and Usenet.

> *Noya: Will you baby-sit my three dogs and four cats this weekend? We're going to the beach.*
> *Jada:* **dts.** *The last time I baby-sat your animals, they ate my books and destroyed my backpack! I won't baby-sit them again until you put them through obedience school.*

See the appendix, pages 189–190, for a complete table of abbreviations. 👁 Look up *chat, e-mail,* and *Usenet.*

duplex printing *Duplex printing* is print-ing on both sides of a sheet of paper. Standard printers require that you enter the sheet of paper twice to print on each of its sides. Duplex printers can print on both sides without the user having to do any-thing. 👁 Look up *printer.*

dust cover Dust and animal fur can dam-age your computer's keyboard, disk drives, and other equipment. A *dust cover* is a thin plastic cover designed to protect your

computer equipment. Use your dust cover only when your computer is turned off. 👁 Look up *disk drive* and *keyboard*.

DVD (**D**igital **V**ersatile **D**isc) A *DVD* is an optical disc similar to a CD-ROM, but with much greater storage capacity. 👁 Look up *CD-ROM*.

Dvorak *Dvorak* is a keyboard layout. It is an alternative to the QWERTY keyboard layout, which is the standard keyboard layout. August Dvorak developed the layout in the 1930s to offer faster typing speeds. The layout is more efficient because, among other things, vowels and the most frequently used consonants are on the home row. The home row is the center row on which the typist keeps his or her fingers initially positioned. This saves the typist from having to reach for frequently used letters. 👁 Look up *home row, keyboard,* and *QWERTY.*

e- *e-* is a prefix that means electronic. Therefore, e-mail means electronic mail. 👁 Look up *e-mail* and *prefix*.

eBay *eBay* is an online auction house that makes it possible for people to buy and sell all types of things through the World Wide Web. It is located at *www.ebay.com*. 👁 Look up *World Wide Web*.

e-book An *e-book* is a book that is provided for readers online or on CD-ROM, rather than on paper.

e-commerce *E-commerce* is short for electronic commerce. E-commerce is business done on the Internet or some other computer network. E-commerce allows you to buy and sell things by using the World Wide Web. The world's largest corporations may someday depend on e-commerce. 👁 Look up *Internet, network,* and *World Wide Web*.

edit When you *edit* a file, you change it so that it becomes more like what you want it to be. 👁 Look up *file*.

editor A computer program that allows the user to create or change an existing file is known as an *editor*. 👁 Look up *file*.

edu *edu* is a top-level Internet domain name that indicates an educational institutional. 👁 Look up *com, net, org,* and *gov*.

EG *EG* is an abbreviation for "evil grin." It is used in informal e-mail, chat, and Usenet. See the appendix, pages 189–190, for a complete table of abbreviations. 👁 Look up *chat, e-mail,* and *Usenet*.

electronic document A document that is meant to be read on a monitor is an *electronic document*. This type of document can use audio and video special effects. A web page is an example of an electronic document. 👁 Look up *web page*.

electronic mailbox An *electronic mailbox* is the place where your e-mail or other electronic messages are held until you access

How has e-mail changed? E-mail has changed quite a bit since it was invented. Today, e-mail messages can be in many different fonts, they can have fancy backgrounds, and you can send files along with e-mail messages. Files that are sent along with an e-mail message are called attachments. Attachments can be picture, word-processor, movie, or other kinds of files. 👁 Look up *acronym, network,* and *word processor.*

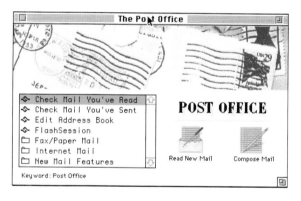

them. If your Internet service uses telephone connections, your messages will be held in the Internet server that you subscribe to until you access the Internet. Then they will be placed into your e-mail mailbox, and you will get a note telling you that you have mail. 👁 Look up *e-mail* and *Internet.*

---

electronic publishing (1) *Electronic publishing* is the business of writing and distributing paperless documents, such *as web pages.*

(2) The use of computerized equipment in the publishing industry is *electronic publishing.*

---

e-mail *E-mail* is an acronym for **electronic mail.**

(1) *E-mail* is a message that you send or receive over a computer network.

(2) To *e-mail* is to send someone a message over a computer network.

---

em dash An *em dash* is a long dash (—). 👁 Look up *dash.*

---

embedded font A font that is part of the file of a formatted document is an *embedded font.* 👁 Look up *font* and *formatting.*

---

emoticon An *emoticon* is a small picture you use to express your feelings about something. Emoticons can be created using only the keys on your keyboard.

When you talk to somebody by e-mail on an online service, you can use emoticons

Table of Emoticons

Emoticon	Meaning
<O> <->	Wink
<O> <O>	Awake
<+> <+>	Unconscious
<-> <->	Asleep
:-)	Smiley face, happy
:)	Smiley face, happy
:-<	Sad face, sad, frown
:(	Sad face, sad
:-(	Sad face, sad
:-o	Surprised
;-)	Wink
:-*	Kiss
:-O	Bored/yawning
I-(	Bored/asleep
>:-(	Angry
:-}	Smirk
B-)	Glasses, cool
:-P	Sticking tongue out
:-D	Laughing, big silly grin
-)	Tongue-in-cheek
=:-)	Nerd
:-)x	Nice dresser
(:-)	Bald head

to show how you feel. 👁 Look up *e-mail, icon, keyboard, online service,* and *Usenet.*

encrypt To *encrypt* means to rearrange data so that it cannot be easily read and understood. To use the data, it must be changed back to its original form. This is called decryption. 👁 Look up *decrypt.*

encryption *Encryption* is the practice of changing information into a code so that only a person with the key or password can understand it. Confidential data that is sent along computer networks is often encrypted.

en dash An *en dash* is a short dash (–). 👁 Look up *dash.*

end user An *end user* is a person who uses a computer system and its software. When you use a computer game or word processor, for example, you are an end user. 👁 Look up *computer, software,* and *word processor.*

Energy Star In order to cut back on the amount of electricity used by personal computers, the U.S. Environmental Protection Agency issued guidelines known as *Energy Star.* A computer that complies with these guidelines uses less electricity when turned on but not in use and switches automatically into a lower power mode if there is no keyboard activity for several minutes.

ergonomics *Ergonomics* is the science of designing equipment to be comfortable and to promote the health of the user. For example, some keyboards are designed with a special shape with the goal of comfort, reduced strain, and other benefits. 👁 Look up *keyboard.*

Warning: Consulting with a physician about the health benefits of any device that claims to be ergonomic would be wise.

error message When you are using an application program, if something goes wrong or if the program needs to warn you about something, you will get an *error message*. If the application program is user-friendly, then the error message will usually explain the problem and tell you how you can solve the problem. 👁 Look up *application program*, *program*, and *user-friendly*.

Esc The *Esc* is the escape key on your keyboard. 👁 Look up *Escape key*.

Escape key The *Escape key* is a key on your keyboard. It looks like [Esc] or [Escape] and is usually at the top left of your keyboard. In most application programs, the escape key lets you stop the program when it is doing something that you do not want it to.

"Mary, this game is playing the introduction again, and I've already seen it a dozen times," John said.

"Just press the escape key to skip the introduction and go straight to the game," Mary told him.

👁 Look up *application program*, *keyboard*, and *program*.

e-tail Selling products and services to consumers by means of the Internet is known as *e-tail* (electronic retail).

Excel *Excel* is a spreadsheet program for Microsoft Windows. 👁 Look up *spreadsheet*.

expansion slot An *expansion slot* is a slot in a computer where you can connect a device that will add to the things that your computer can do. For example, to install a modem into your computer, you may install a modem card into an expansion slot on the motherboard inside of your computer. 👁 Look up *card, modem,* and *motherboard.*

expert system An *expert system* is a program that contains the knowledge of an expert in some field, such as engineering or medicine. The system uses that knowledge to form conclusions. Many people would say that expert systems are an exam-

ple of artificial intelligence. 👁 Look up *artificial intelligence* and *program.*

extension In computer file names, an *extension* is a group of letters or symbols at the end of the file name that denotes the type of file. For example, the suffix .jpg in the file name

myself.jpg

means that the file is a JPEG image, which you can view. 👁 Look up *file, gif, image, JPEG,* and *wav.*

e-zine A magazine that is published electronically is known as an *e-zine.* 👁 Look up *electronic publishing.*

F2F *F2F* is an abbreviation for "face to face." It is used in informal e-mail, chat, and Usenet.

> *John: Let's meet f2f.*
> *Paul: OK, come by my house at 7:00 P.M. tomorrow.*

See the appendix, pages 189–190, for a complete table of abbreviations. 👁 Look up *chat, e-mail,* and *Usenet.*

FAQ *FAQ* is an acronym for **f**requently **a**sked **q**uestions. Very often when you use new software or view a new web site, you will have questions. Who made the program or site? What is its purpose? How do I do certain things with it? You can find answers to these and other questions in the FAQ. 👁 Look up *program, software,* and *web site.*

favorite In Microsoft Internet Explorer, a *favorite* is the name of a web site that you have visited and plan to visit again. Favorites are listed in the Favorites folder. 👁 Look up *web site.*

Favorites folder In Microsoft Internet Explorer, the *Favorites folder* lets you store the names and URLs of web sites that you have visited and will return to. When you click on the Favorites file, your computer will display a file with all the sites you have selected. All you have to do is click on the one you want. 👁 Look up *folder, Microsoft Internet Explorer, URL,* and *web site.*

fax modem A *fax modem* is a circuit board that functions as a modem but also allows you to send fax messages. 👁 Look up *circuit board* and *modem.*

feature A *feature* is a part of a program that does a specific job. For example, a spell checker is a feature of most word processors.

Do I have to use all the features of a program? No. For example, most current word-processing programs allow you to choose which features you want to use.

fiber optics Large amounts of information can be sent at high speeds using *fiber optics* because cables filled with fibers or glass allow light to transmit data.  Look up *data, DSL, information,* and *Internet.*

field A *field* is a space that you use to enter information into a database, a spreadsheet, or a form. The space is displayed on your monitor. Look up *database, form,* and *spreadsheet.*

file A *file* is a collection of data that a computer can use for some purpose. When you

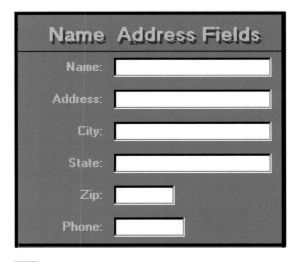

Name Address Fields

Name:
Address:
City:
State:
Zip:
Phone:

use computers, you use files all the time. When you write a letter using a word processor, your letter is stored as a file. web pages are files. Software programs are files, so when you play a video game, you are using a file. When you download movies or music from web sites, you are downloading files. Look up *data, download, software program, web site,* and *Word processor.*

filename The name of a file is its *filename.*

file size The *file size* of a file tells you how big the file is. It is usually given in bytes. Look up *byte* and *file.*

file transfer *File transfer* is the act of copying a file from one computer to another. Just as people can give physical files to each other, computers can give electronic files to each other. 👁 Look up *file*.

file transfer protocol (ftp) *File transfer protocol (ftp)* is any system for transferring files between computers. File transfer protocol is used, for example, when you transfer files over the Internet. 👁 Look up *file* and *Internet*.

fix A solution to a flaw in a software program is a *fix*. Usually a corrected version of the program is issued to correct the problem. 👁 Look up *software program*.

F keys 👁 Look up *function keys*.

flatbed scanner This is a type of scanner in which the object being scanned is held flat against a piece of glass. 👁 Look up *scanner*.

floppy *Floppy* usually means a 3½-inch or a 5¼-inch diskette. 👁 Look up *diskette*.

floppy disk *Floppy disk* means a 3½-inch or a 5¼-inch diskette. 👁 Look up *diskette*.

flush Material that is *flush* is flat against the margin. 👁 Look up *flush left* and *flush right*.

flush left *Flush left* is a way of arranging text so that each line starts at the same left edge. The left margin is aligned, but the right edge is irregular. 👁 Look up *align, flush,* and *flush right*.

*This sentence
is an example of text
that is set flush left.*

flush right *Flush right* is a way of arranging text so that each line of text ends at the same right edge. The beginning of each line is irregular, but the right margin is aligned. 👁 Look up *align, flush,* and *flush left*.

*This sentence is an
example of text that
is set flush right.*

folder A *folder* is a collection of files. Folders are used to organize files. 👁 Look up *file*.

font A *font* is a collection of upper and lower case letters, numbers, punctuation, and popular symbols in the same style and size.

font size The *font size* of a font is roughly the distance from the bottom of a descender to the top of an ascender. The font size is usually expressed in points. 👁 Look up *ascender, descender,* and *point.*

6 point

8 point

10 point

12 point

18 point

24 point

36 point

48 point

72 point

font style *Font style* is the design of a font.

1. **Cooper Black**
2. Cheltenham
3. **Tekton Bold**
4. **Chicago**
5. 𝕸𝖆𝖗𝖎𝖆𝖌𝖊
6. *Ingenius*
7. *Kaufmann*
8. Copperplate
9. **Impress**
10. **Garamond Ultra**

foot The bottom of the page is the *foot.* 👁 Look up *head.*

footer A *footer* is a special line of text and/or other items at the bottom of a

word-processing document. For example, a footer may contain the page number, date, or notes. 👁 Look up *header* and *word processor.*

form A *form* is part of a web page that lets you enter information. 👁 Look up *field, information,* and *web page.*

format (1) A *format* is an arrangement of information. For example, a word processor uses a format to arrange the letters, words, and symbols that you enter when you type a document. 👁 Look up *information* and *word processor.*

(2) To *format* a disk is to place a magnetic pattern onto a disk so that it will be able to store data. 👁 Look up *data, disk, information, symbol,* and *word processor.*

formatting A file has *formatting* when it has a special structure that tells the computer how to use the information in the file. For example, a word processor file for a letter to your aunt will contain the text of the letter, but it will also contain formatting that tells the computer the font, font size, margins, and so on. 👁 Look up *file, font size, information,* and *word processing.*

Forward button The *Forward button* is a button on most web browsers. If you used the Back button to return to a web page that you already viewed, you can use the Forward button to return to the page you were viewing. 👁 Look up *Back button, browser, Home button, Stop button,* and *web page.*

forward slash (/) The *forward slash* is one of the symbols on your keyboard. It is on the same key as the question mark (?). The forward has many uses. It is used, for example, in dates such as 12/25/00 and in the names of World Wide Web documents. 👁 Look up *backslash, keyboard, symbol,* and *World Wide Web.*

1/09/01

http://www.barronseduc.com

fps *fps* is an abbreviation for **f**rames **p**er **s**econd. fps is a measure of the number of frames shown per second in a video clip. 👁 Look up *video clip.*

fragmented A file is *fragmented* if it is stored on a disk in an inefficient way. A fragmented file is broken up and stored in many small pieces, or fragments, scattered around the disk. If a disk is fragmented, then files on the disk are fragmented. Your computer will take longer to access files from a fragmented disk. 👁 Look up *access, data, disk,* and *file.*

frame rate The *frame rate* of a video clip is the number of frames displayed per second. The higher the frame rate, the higher the quality of the video clip. Frame rate is measured in fps, which means frames per second.  Look up *fps* and *video clip.*

freeware Software that can be legally copied and given free of charge to other users is *freeware.*

FTP *FTP* is an abbreviation for **f**ile **t**ransfer **p**rotocol. It is a set of rules that computers follow when they are exchanging files over the Internet. Look up *file* and *Internet.*

ftp *ftp* is an abbreviation for **f**ile **t**ransfer **p**rotocol. File transfer protocol is a way of sending data from one computer to another. Look up c*omputer* and *data.*

function keys The keys labeled F1 to F12 are *function keys* or F keys. They perform different functions depending on the software you are running. Look up *software.*

FWIW *FWIW* is an abbreviation for "for what it is worth." It is used in informal e-mail, chat, and Usenet.

> John: *fwiw, I think that movie was bad.*
> Paul: *I agree.*

See the appendix, pages 189–190, for a complete table of abbreviations. Look up *chat, e-mail,* and *Usenet.*

FYI *FYI* is an abbreviation for "for your information." It is used in informal e-mail, chat, and Usenet.

> John: *I didn't know that you and Susan were best friends.*
> Jane: **fyi,** *we've been best friends for four years.*

See the appendix, pages 189–190, for a complete table of abbreviations. Look up *chat, e-mail,* and *Usenet.*

G2G *G2G* is an abbreviation for "got to go." It is used in informal e-mail, chat, and Usenet.

> *Paul:* **g2g**, *or I'll be late for my soccer game.*
> *Juan: Bye.*

See the appendix, pages 189–190, for a complete table of abbreviations. 👁 Look up *chat, e-mail,* and *Usenet.*

G3 The *G3* is a series of Macintosh computers. 👁 Look up *computer* and *Macintosh.*

G4 The *G4* is a series of Macintosh computers. 👁 Look up *computer* and *Macintosh.*

gamma The brightness of a picture is controlled by the *gamma* setting. For example,

many paint and draw programs allow you to control the gamma setting of a picture. 👁 Look up *draw program* and *paint program.*

gamma testing *Gamma testing* is the third test of software. Gamma testing is done after beta testing but before the software is sold to computer users. Gamma testing is named after gamma (γ), the third letter of the Greek alphabet. 👁 Look up *alpha testing, beta testing, computer user, Greek alphabet,* and *software.*

garbage in, garbage out *Garbage in, garbage out* is the idea that the work that a computer does is only as good as the information that it is given. If bad information is input into a computer, then the output will be worthless.

Gates, (William H.) Bill (1955–) *Bill Gates* began Microsoft in 1977. He developed DOS, the operating system of IBM computers. He was Chairman and CEO of Microsoft Corporation until 1999, when he became Chief Software Architect. In 1999, Mr. Gates was the richest individual

in the world. His fortune was about 100 billion dollars. Without a doubt, he is one of the most important people of our time. 👁 Look up *IBM, Microsoft Corporation,* and *operating system.*

gateway A *gateway* is a link between different computer networks.

GFETE *GFETE* is an abbreviation for "grinning from ear to ear." It is used in informal e-mail, chat, and Usenet. See the appendix, pages 189–190, for a complete table of abbreviations. 👁 Look up *chat, e-mail,* and *Usenet.*

GG *GG* is an abbreviation for "gotta' go." It is used in informal e-mail, chat, and Usenet.

Mary: My friend just got here and were going to go swimming. **gg.**
Jane: OK. Bye.

See the appendix, pages 189–190, for a complete table of abbreviations. 👁 Look up *chat, e-mail,* and *Usenet.*

ghosting If you leave a computer on for a long time with the same image on the screen, the image may remain after you turn the computer off. This is called *ghosting.* Ghosting happens because the image has caused damage to the screen in the shape of the image. Ghosting is not as much of a problem with current monitors as it was with older computers. Screen savers are often used to prevent ghosting. Ghosting is sometimes called burn-in. 👁 Look up *burn-in, image, screen,* and *screen saver.*

GIF (pronounced jif) *Gif* is a data compression format for compressing pictures.  Look up *data compression, file,* and *JPEG.*

gif *gif* is an extension that indicates that a file is a GIF image file. Look up *extension, file, GIF,* and *image.*

gig (rhymes with "big") *Gig* is an informal word for gigabyte. A gigabyte is about one billion (1,000,000,000) bytes of information. Look up *byte* and *information.*

giga- *giga-* is a prefix meaning one billion (1,000,000,000). In computer and Internet terminology, it means 1,073,741,824 (which equals 2^{30}). Look up *gigabyte, kilobyte,* and *megabyte.*

gigabyte A *gigabyte* is about one billion (1,000,000,000) bytes of information. (It is exactly 1,073,741,824 bytes.) Look up *byte, information, kilobyte,* and *megabyte.*

gigahertz *gigahertz* means one billion (1,000,000,000) Hz. Look up *Hz.*

GIGO *GIGO* is an acronym for garbage in, garbage out. Look up *acronym* and *garbage in, garbage out.*

glitch A *glitch* takes place when a computer responds incorrectly because signals that should arrive at the same time arrive at slightly different times.

GMTA *GMTA* is an abbreviation for "great minds think alike." It is used in informal e-mail, chat, and Usenet. See the appendix, pages 189–190, for a complete table of abbreviations. Look up *chat, e-mail,* and *Usenet.*

google A *google* is equal to the number 1 followed by 100 zeros. When written out, the google looks like this:

10,000,000,000,000,000,000,00
0,000,000,000,000,000,000,000,
000,000,000,000,000,000,000,0
00,000,000,000,000,000,000,00
0,000,000,000,000.

A google can also be written as 10^{100}.
👁 Look up *googleplex.*

. . . .

googleplex A *googleplex* is equal to the number 1 followed by a google of zeros.
👁 Look up *google.*

. . . .

gov *gov* is a top-level Internet domain name that indicates a government office or a government agency. 👁 Look up *com, edu, net,* and *org.*

. . . .

grabhandles 👁 Look up *handles.*

. . . .

graphical user interface (GUI) When you use your computer, you can work with software, select files, and so on by clicking on images called icons. The program that lets you do this is the *graphical user interface.* (GUI is the acronym for graphical user interface and is pronounced G—U—I or "gooey.") The Apple Macintosh was the first personal computer to use a graphical user interface.

How did people use computers before graphical user interfaces? Before computers had GUIs, you had to type in commands to work with the computer. For example, to run a program called Blaster Master, you may have had to type something like

run blastermaster

instead of just clicking on the icon for the game. Most IBM-compatible computers use a GUI called Microsoft Windows. 👁 Look up *computer, click, command, file, icon, Macintosh, Microsoft Windows,* and *software.*

. . . .

gram A *gram* is a metric unit of mass equal to one-thousandth (1/1000) of a kilogram or 0.002 pounds.

. . . .

graphics *Graphics* are the images that you see on your computer screen. 👁 Look up *computer.*

. . . .

grayed A menu option that appears in light gray rather than black type cannot be selected. A menu selection is *grayed* when it is impossible to perform its function. For example, the options to close or save a document will be grayed if no document has been opened. 👁 Look up *dimmed.*

. . . .

Greek alphabet The *Greek alphabet* is the alphabet of the Greek language. Letters from the Greek alphabet are used in physics, mathematics, and many other sciences. Here is the Greek alphabet and the names of the letters.

Notice that Greek letters have an uppercase and a lowercase just like English letters do.

Greek Letter	Name
A α	alpha
B β	beta
Γ γ	gamma
Δ δ	delta
E ε	epsilon
Z ζ	zeta
H η	eta
Θ θ	theta
I ι	iota
K κ	kappa
Λ λ	lambda
M μ	mu
N ν	nu
Ξ ξ	xi
O o	omicron
Π π	pi
P ρ	rho
Σ σ	sigma
T τ	tau
Y υ	upsilon
Φ φ	phi
X χ	chi
Ψ ψ	psi
Ω ω	omega

As you use computers and the Internet, you will no doubt see the Greek alphabet used. For example, *alpha testing* and *gamma* are terms that use Greek letters. Also, when you learn about mathematics and science by using the Internet, you will see Greek letters used. ◉ Look up *alpha testing, gamma,* and *Internet.*

GTG *GTG* is an abbreviation for "got to go." It is used in informal e-mail, chat, and Usenet. See the appendix, pages 189–190, for a complete table of abbreviations. ◉ Look up *chat, e-mail,* and *Usenet.*

GUI *GUI* (pronounced G—U—I or "gooey") is an acronym for **g**raphical **u**ser **i**nterface. ◉ Look up *graphical user interface.*

gutter The blank space between columns of type or between pages of a book is the *gutter.*

hack When adventurers travel through dark and dangerous jungles in search of treasure or lost cities, they have to make their own paths. They *hack* their way through the vines with machetes to reach their goal. Obstacles sometimes keep computer programmers from their goals. When you are talking about computers, hack has all of the following meanings.

(1) To find a clever solution to a computer problem that gives unbelievably good results and shows that the problem solver may just be an utter genius!

(2) To make something work by a trick without careful planning.

(3) To try to get access to a computer, a computer network, a program, or a web site without permission. 👁 Look up *access, network, program, programmer,* and *web site.*

hacker A *hacker* is a person who tries to get access to a computer, a computer network, a program, or a web site without permission. 👁 Look up *access, network, program,* and *web site.*

hand scanner A *hand scanner* is an optical scanner operated by hand. A hand scanner is held by its handle. It is dragged over the material to be scanned into the computer. 👁 Look up *computer, drag,* and *scanner.*

hard copy A *hard copy* is a printout of a file onto paper.

> "Dad, can I use the printer?" John asked. I need to make a **hard copy** of my history report."
> "As soon as I'm finished, son. I'm making a **hard copy** of a report for work," John's father said.

👁 Look up *file*.

handshaking The signals exchanged between two computers to show that data transmission is proceeding properly is known as *handshaking*.

handle A *handle* is a name, other than your own, by which you are known in chat, in a BBS, or in some other system when you communicate with other people. 👁 Look up *BBS, chat,* and *communicate.*

handles *Handles* are small boxes that you use to resize, rescale, or move an image that you are making with a draw program. 👁 Look up *draw program.*

Happy Mac The *Happy Mac* is the happy face that you see on a Macintosh when it starts running and everything is OK. 👁 Look up *Sad Mac* and *Macintosh.*

hard disk 👁 Look up *hard drive.*

hard drive A *hard drive* is a data storage drive with a hard disk inside a sealed box. The hard drive is usually mounted inside your computer.

How much data can a hard drive store? A hard drive can store much more information than a floppy disk. The storage capacity of current hard disks is from 4.3 to 47 gigabytes of data. One gigabyte is about one billion (1,000,000,000) bytes, or about 695 1.44-MB 3½-inch floppy disks. 👁 Look up *data, floppy disk,* and *information.*

hard edge A *hard edge* is an edge that is sharp, with no blurring of the boundary. 👁 Look up *soft edge.*

hard page A forced page break, where the word processor must start a new page whether or not the preceding page is full, is a *hard page.* 👁 Look up *word processor.*

hardware *Hardware* is the part of a computer system that can be seen and touched. For example, a disk drive can be seen and touched, so it is hardware. 👁 Look up *computer system* and *disk drive.*

head (1) The HTML *<HEAD>* tag shows where the heading of a web page begins.
(2) The top of a page is the head. 👁 Look up *<BODY>* and *foot.*

header A *header* is a special line of text and/or other items at the top of a word-processing document. For example, a header may contain the title or chapter heading and date. 👁 Look up *footer* and *word processor.*

heading A *heading* is a line of text that names a block of text. Headings are used in web pages to tell you what a section of text is about. 👁 Look up *text* and *web page.*

Help Programs often have a *Help* feature that you can use when you are having difficulty using the program. The word *Help* often appears on a menu bar. You can select help by clicking on the word *Help.* Most Help features allow you to choose from a list of topics or type the topic that you want help with. 👁 Look up *click, feature, menu bar,* and *program.*

Hertz 👁 Look up *Hz.*

Hewlett-Packard *Hewlett-Packard* is well-known manufacturer of computers and printers. You can learn about Hewlett-Packard at *http://www.hp.com.*

hexadecimal *Hexadecimal* is a system for counting based on the symbols 0, 1, 2, 3, 4, 5, 6, 7, 8, 9, *A, B, C, D, E,* and *F.* Our way of counting, base ten, or decimal numbers, does not work well with the binary system that computers use for their internal operations. The hexadecimal system is used because it does work well with the internal operations of computers. The table shown gives the hexadecimal numbers from 0 to 31.

Decimal	Hexadecimal	Decimal	Hexadecimal
0	0	16	10
1	1	17	11
2	2	18	12
3	3	19	13
4	4	20	14
5	5	21	15
6	6	22	16
7	7	23	17
8	8	24	18
9	9	25	19
10	A	26	1A
11	B	27	1B
12	C	28	1C
13	D	29	1D
14	E	30	1E
15	F	31	1F

👁 Look up *binary numbers* and *symbol.*

hidden file A *hidden file* is a file that is not visible on the usual menus. Some operating system files are hidden so that they cannot be erased by mistake. 👁 Look up *menu* and *operating system.*

high-density disk A *high-density disk* stores a great amount of information. A high-density disk holds many more bytes than a double-density disk. A 3½-inch high-density diskette holds 1,440,000 bytes (1.44 MB) of information. 👁 Look up *byte, information,* and *MB.*

highlight A *highlighted* menu item is made either darker or lighter to indicate that it has been selected.

History The *History* is a feature on most browsers that displays a list of links that you have visited. 👁 Look up *browser* and *hyperlink.*

hit A *hit* is a visit to a web page. Many web sites have counters that keep a count of the number of hits that they receive.

Home button The *Home button* is a button on most web browsers that takes you back to the first web page that appears when you begin using your web browser. 👁 Look up *Back button, browser, Forward button, Stop button,* and *web page.*

home computer A *home computer* is a computer made for use in your home.

Home key The *Home key* is the key on a computer keyboard that moves the cursor to the same place each time it is pressed, usually the top left corner. 👁 Look up *computer* and *keyboard.*

home page A *home page* is the main page of a web site, which users read first to see what other pages of the site they want to access. 👁 Look up *web site.*

home row The *home row* of a keyboard is the center row of the keyboard. As a typist types, he or she returns the fingers to the home row. On standard keyboards (called QWERTY keyboards), the letters A, S, D, F, G, H, J, K, and L appear on the home row. 👁 Look up *Dvorak, keyboard,* and *QWERTY.*

horizontal Something that is *horizontal* runs from side to side or across. 👁 Look up *vertical.*

horizontal scrolling When you are looking at an image that is too big to fit into a window, you can use scrolling to see all of the image. *Horizontal scrolling* means moving the image side to side. This shows the hidden parts of the image on the left and right sides. It is usually done by using the scroll bar at the bottom of the window (or by using the horizontal scrolling wheel on your mouse if you have a mouse with scrolling wheels). 👁 Look up *image, mouse, scroll, scroll bar, scrolling wheel, vertical scrolling* and *window.*

host A *host* is a computer on the Internet that is the source of files or the destination of files. The host keeps the information party going! 👁 Look up *computer, file,* and *Internet.*

hot list A *hot list* is a list of web addresses, bookmarks, or favorites that are important to the user. 👁 Look up *bookmark* and *favorite.*

hot spot The exact part of a pointer or mouse curser that must touch an option in order to select it is the *hot spot.*

hot zone The *hot zone* is that section at the end of a typed line that causes the computer to hyphenate words. If a word is in the hot zone it will be hyphenated to make it fit on the line.

hourglass icon In Microsoft Windows, the cursor takes the shape of an *hourglass* during the time the computer is working and cannot accept any commands from the keyboard. The hourglass turns over and over while the computer is busy working. The cursor resumes its regular shape when the computer is ready to respond to new commands.

HTH *HTH* is an abbreviation for "hope this helps." It is used in informal e-mail, chat, and Usenet.

> *Marcy: I am supposed to bring chocolate-chip cookies to the bake sale tomorrow, and I don't have a recipe. Pam:* **hth.** *I am e-mailing you my favorite chocolate-chip cookie recipe. Good luck!*

See the appendix, pages 189–190, for a complete table of abbreviations. 👁 Look up *chat, e-mail,* and *Usenet.*

HTML *HTML* is an acronym for **H**yper**t**ext **M**arkup **L**anguage. HTML is used to make documents on the World Wide Web. 👁 Look up *hypertext* and *World Wide Web.*

hyperlink A *hyperlink* is a word, an image, or anything else on a web page that you can click on to go to another web page or to another place in the same web page. Hyperlinks are usually underlined and colored. Images that are hyperlinks usually have a blue border. Hyperlinks are also called links. 👁 Look up *click* and *web page.*

How can I find out who my favorite college football team will play this weekend? First, go to a sports web site. Then click on football. When you get to the football page, click on schedule. On the schedule page, scroll to your team, and click on the link. The next page should tell you who the team is playing that weekend. You could also go to the college's web site and follow the hyperlinks.

hypertext *Hypertext* lets you prepare and publish text so that a reader can choose his or her own paths through it by clicking on hyperlinks. 👁 Look up *click, hyperlink,* and *text.*

Hz *Hz* is an abbreviation for Hertz. If something happens at 1 Hz, then it happens 1 time every second. The prefix M- stands for mega, which means 1,000,000. So, megahertz, or MHz, means one million (1,000,000) Hz, or that something is happening 1,000,000 times every second. Hertz are used to measure a computer's clock speed, which determines how fast a computer runs. For example, a 330 MHz machine runs almost four times faster than a 90 MHz machine. 👁 Look up *computer.*

<I> tag   The *<I> tag* is an HTML tag that makes italic type.   Look up *HTML, italic,* and *tag.*

IANAL   *IANAL* is an abbreviation for "I am not a lawyer." It is used in informal e-mail, chat, and Usenet. See the appendix, pages 189–190, for a complete table of abbreviations.   Look up *chat, e-mail,* and *Usenet.*

iBook   The *iBook* is the laptop version of the iMac computer.   Look up *computer, iMac,* and *laptop computer.*

IBM   *IBM* is an abbreviation for **I**nternational **B**usiness **M**achines. IBM is a leading maker of computers. The IBM PC is one of the two main types of personal computers.   Look up *personal computer.*

IBM-compatible   An *IBM-compatible* computer is a computer made to the same specifications as an IBM PC but by a company other than IBM. IBM-compatible computers are designed to run the same programs and to use the same devices as an IBM PC.   Look up *device.*

ICCL   *ICCL* is an abbreviation for "I could care less." It is used in informal e-mail, chat, and Usenet.

Mary: Jane says that Juan is the best soccer player on the team.
*Noya: **iccl**. I still believe that Mike "El Spider" Johnson is the best.*

See the appendix, pages 189–190, for a complete table of abbreviations. 👁 Look up *chat, e-mail,* and *Usenet.*

-----

icon An *icon* is a small picture. Icons usually stand for a program, a file, or a command. On computers with a graphical user interface (GUI), you point to icons using a mouse, or some other pointing device, and click on them to run programs or perform commands. 👁 Look up *graphical user interface, mouse, pointing device* and *program.*

IE *IE* is an abbreviation for Internet Explorer. 👁 Look up *Microsoft Internet Explorer.*

IIRC *IIRC* is an abbreviation for "if I remember correctly." It is used in informal e-mail, chat, and Usenet.

Jane: I hear you are making cookies.
Mary: That's right. I forgot how many cups of flour to use, though.
*Jane: **iirc**, it's 2 cups.*

See the appendix, pages 189–190, for a complete table of abbreviations. 👁 Look up *chat, e-mail,* and *Usenet.*

-----

illegal operation An *illegal operation* occurs when a program performs an operation that it is not allowed to perform. Illegal operations are usually the result of programming errors. 👁 Look up *program.*

IM *IM* is the abbreviation for "instant message."

Mathew: You can't leave yet. We haven't finished making plans for our trip.
*Allan: I have to run out to do some errands. I'll **im** you as soon as I get back and we can finish planning.*

See the appendix, pages 189–190, for a complete table of abbreviations.

-----

iMac The *iMac* is the latest version of the Macintosh computer. The original Macintosh computer was introduced in 1984 by Apple Computer, Incorporated.

👁 Look up *Apple Computer, Incorporated* and *Macintosh*.

....

image An *image* is a picture that you see on a computer monitor. 👁 Look up *computer* and *monitor*.

....

<IMG> tag The *<IMG> tag* is an HTML tag used to put an image into a web page. 👁 Look up *HTML, image, tag,* and *web page*.

....

IMHO *IMHO* is an abbreviation for "in my humble opinion." It is used in informal e-mail, chat, and Usenet.

> Juan: **imho**, *I don't think that you should play sports this year if your knee doesn't heal.*
> Paul: *Thanks for your concern.*

See the appendix, pages 189–190, for a complete table of abbreviations. 👁 Look up *chat, e-mail,* and *Usenet.*

....

IMO *IMO* is an abbreviation for "in my opinion." It is used in informal e-mail, chat, and Usenet.

> Jane: *I think everyone should have to read a book a week so that they will become smarter.*
> Mary: *Good idea. However,* **imo**, *not many people would do that.*

See the appendix, pages 189–190, for a complete table of abbreviations. 👁 Look up *chat, e-mail,* and *Usenet.*

....

inactive A menu item or feature that you cannot select and use is *inactive*. An item that you can select and use is active. Inactive items in a menu usually appear in a lighter color than that of active items so that you will know they are inactive. 👁 Look up *active, feature,* and *menu.*

....

include To *include* a message or a file means to add a message or a file (usually as an enclosure) to a message that you send to another person. 👁 Look up *e-mail* and *file.*

....

infected A disk, program, or file that contains a virus is *infected*. Viruses can damage your computer, so you should not use infected items. 👁 Look up *antivirus program, disk, file, program,* and *virus.*

....

information Any set of symbols, sounds, sights, patterns, or anything else that means something to somebody is *information*. There are many examples of information.

Your name and address are information. When you talk with your best friend over the telephone and your voice is carried to your friend, what you say is information. The data stored on a CD-ROM that your computer uses to play your favorite video game is information. The light that astronomers receive from distant stars gives them information about the stars.

Information is very important in the world of computers and the Internet. Computers are tools that use and work with information. The Internet allows people to share information. 👁 Look up *CD-ROM* and *video game.*

information superhighway The *information superhighway* is an informal name for

the Internet, the network of computers that links people to each other and to sources of information. 👁 Look up *information* and *network.*

inkjet printer An *inkjet printer* is a printer that prints by spraying a jet of ink onto paper. 👁 Look up *laser printer* and *printer.*

input device An *input device* is anything that you use to put information into a computer. For example, a keyboard, a mouse, a trackball, and a scanner are all input devices. 👁 Look up *information, keyboard, mouse,* and *trackball.*

insertion point The place on the computer screen where letters or characters will appear when you start typing is the *insertion point.* This point is indicated with a cursor or blinking vertical bar. 👁 Look up *cursor* and *mouse pointer.*

install To *install* is to put into or to make a part of. For example, to play a game on a computer, you have to install the game. Most programs have to be installed before they can be used. The instructions that come with software programs should explain how to install the software. 👁 Look up *program* and *software program.*

installation program 👁 Look up *setup program.*

instruction manual An *instruction manual* is a book or set of papers that explains how to set up and use a computer system or any part of a computer system. ◉ Look up *computer system*.

integrated circuit (IC) An *integrated circuit (IC)* is a rectangular piece of material with a circuit inside. Integrated circuits make up the CPU and memory of your computer. ◉ Look up *computer, CPU,* and *memory*.

Intel *Intel* is the largest maker of microprocessors. Intel made the 8088, 286, 386, and 486 microprocessor. They also make the Pentium, Pentium Pro, Pentium II, and Pentium III processors. The CPUs of most computers are made by Intel, although other companies make microprocessors to compete with Intel. ◉ Look up *CPU* and *microprocessor*.

interactive *Interactive* means that you can do things and the computer will respond to what you do. For example, a web page that lets you make specific choices, lets you do specific things, and responds to your actions is interactive. ◉ Look up *web page*.

interface (1) To *interface* is to exchange information in some way. When you type on a computer keyboard or use a mouse, for example, you are interfacing.

(2) An *interface* is the way that a program communicates with its user. ◉ Look up *communicate, information, keyboard, mouse,* and *program*.

internal font An *internal font* is a font built into your printer. It contains all the information about a set of letters, numbers, and symbols. Your printer uses this information to print documents. ◉ Look up *font* and *printer*.

International Business Machines Corporation ◉ Look up *IBM*.

Internet The *Internet* is a system of computer networks. It links computers around the world. The Internet lets computer users share files, send and receive e-mail, use the World Wide Web, and do many other things. You can use the Internet to learn about butterflies or the planet Jupiter, talk with others about things that interest you, send e-mail to a friend, and do many other things. You can also buy things, but you

connections. The World Wide Web, on the other hand, is a collection of hypertext documents stored on servers.

👁 Look up *e-mail, file, hypertext, network, server,* and *World Wide Web.*

Internet Explorer 👁 Look up *Microsoft Internet Explorer.*

Internet Explorer 3.0 *Internet Explorer 3.0* was an early version of Microsoft Internet Explorer, which is Microsoft's web browser. 👁 Look up *browser* and *Microsoft Corporation.*

Internet Explorer 4.0 *Internet Explorer 4.0* is a version of Microsoft Internet Explorer, which is Microsoft's web browser. It is a powerful improvement over Internet Explorer 3.0. 👁 Look up *browser* and *Microsoft Corporation.*

Internet service provider (ISP) An *Internet service provider (ISP)* is a company that connects you to the Internet. Most ISPs charge a monthly fee for their service. 👁 Look up *Internet.*

interword spacing *Interword spacing,* or wordspacing, is the space between words.

intranet An *intranet* is a network used by a single organization. The network is

would certainly want to talk with your parents before doing that.

Why was the Internet invented? The Internet began when scientists wanted to communicate with each other and read one another's work. With the help of the government, a network called the ARPANET was made. The Internet developed from this network.

Why are people so excited about the Internet? The Internet allows people to do many things that are important to them. It allows people to communicate, learn, shop, and many other things. Also, for the first time in history, people all around the world are able to communicate directly and inexpensively.

What is the difference between the Internet and the World Wide Web? The Internet is a collection of computers and not accessible to anyone outside the organization.

⋯⋯⋯⋯⋯⋯⋯⋯⋯⋯⋯⋯

I/O (pronounced "eye-oh") *I/O* stands for **i**nput and **o**utput. Most of the time when you use a computer, you are either putting information into it (input) or getting information from it (output). So, except for when it is computing something, a computer spends much of its time on input and output. I/O is the part of your computer that lets it input information and output information. This includes input devices like the keyboard and mouse and output devices like the monitor and printer. ◉ Look up *computer* and *information*.

⋯⋯⋯⋯⋯⋯⋯⋯⋯⋯⋯⋯

Iomega *Iomega* is the manufacturer of Zip and Jaz drives. It is located on the web at *http://www.iomega.com.* ◉ Look up *disk drive, Jaz drive,* and *Zip drive.*

⋯⋯⋯⋯⋯⋯⋯⋯⋯⋯⋯⋯

IOW *IOW* is the abbreviation for "in other words." It is used in informal e-mail, chat, and Usenet.

> *Stephanie: Monday is a very busy day for me. I have to water my plants, bathe the dog, pay the bills, roll up my spare change....*
> *Bob: **iow** you don't want to help me move.*
> *Stephanie: How could you tell?*

See the appendix, pages 189–190, for a complete table of abbreviations. ◉ Look up *chat, e-mail,* and *Usenet.*

⋯⋯⋯⋯⋯⋯⋯⋯⋯⋯⋯⋯

IP address *IP address* is short for **I**nternet **P**rotocol address. An IP address is an Internet address in numeric form. This type of address differs from a domain address, which is in readable form. ◉ Look up *domain address.*

⋯⋯⋯⋯⋯⋯⋯⋯⋯⋯⋯⋯

IRL *IRL* is an abbreviation for "in real life." It is used in informal e-mail, chat, and Usenet.

> *Mary: What do you do **irl**?*
> *Paul: I am a student.*

See the appendix, pages 189–190, or a complete table of abbreviations. ◉ Look up *chat, e-mail,* and *Usenet.*

⋯⋯⋯⋯⋯⋯⋯⋯⋯⋯⋯⋯

ISO *ISO* is an abbreviation for "in search of." It is used in informal e-mail, chat, and Usenet.

> *Jane: I am **iso** some chocolate chip cookie dough to make cookies for my slumber party tonight.*
> *Mary: No problem. I can bring some.*

See the appendix, pages 189–190, for a complete table of abbreviations. 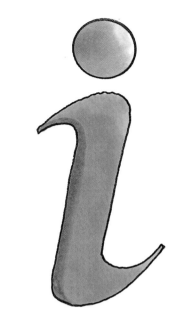 Look up *chat, e-mail,* and *Usenet.*

ISP *ISP* is an abbreviation for **I**nternet **se**rvice **p**rovider. 👁 Look up *Internet service provider.*

IT *IT* is the abbreviation for **i**nformation **t**echnology. Information technology is the technology related to computers and electronic communication.

italic Type that is slanted is *italic* type. Italic type has many uses. For example, you can use italics when you want people to know that a word is important.

This is an example of a normal font
This is an example of an italic font

iway *Iway* is the abbreviation for the information superhighway. 👁 Look up *information superhighway.*

jack A *jack* is an electrical connector into which a plug can be inserted.

jargon *Jargon* is a special word or group of words that are used by people in the know to talk about a particular thing. For example, RAM (random-access memory) and ROM (read-only memory) are examples of computer jargon. Another example is boot. To boot a computer is to start it, while in normal English, boots are things that you wear on your feet! 👁 Look up *boot, RAM,* and *ROM.*

Java *Java* is a programming language. What makes Java special is that it can run on many different kinds of computers. Java programs can be downloaded to your computer when you use a web browser. These programs can do many things. For example, a Java program can make an animation on your screen. 👁 Look up *animation, browser, computer program, download, programming language, screen,* and *World Wide Web.*

JavaScript To write web sites that are interactive, web page designers use *JavaScript.* JavaScript is a programming language that your browser can read.

👁 Look up *browser, interactive, programming language, web design, web page,* and *web site.*

Jaz drive A *Jaz drive* is a type of disk drive made by Iomega Corporation. 👁 Look up *disk* and *disk drive.*

jewel case A *jewel case* is a case for storing CDs. 👁 Look up *compact disc.*

Jobs, Stephen (Paul) (1955–) *Stephen Jobs* is the founder of Apple Computer, Incorporated along with Stephen "The Woz" Wozniak.

joystick A *joystick* is a pointing device that has a handle attached to a base. The base is

connected to the computer by a cable. The handle is pushed, pulled, or turned to the front, to the back, and to either side of the base. The handle makes an arrow, a spaceship, a knight, or some other object on the screen move. The object will keep moving in the direction the handle is pointed. Joysticks are often used to play game programs. 👁 Look up *pointing device* and *program*.

JPEG (pronounced "jay-peg") *JPEG* is an acronym for Joint Photographic Experts Group. It is a file format for compressing pictures. Pictures usually take up a lot of memory. JPEG compresses them so that they do not take up so much space. Many of the pictures you see on your computer or download from a web site are compressed using JPEG.

jpg *jpg* is an extension that indicates that a file is a JPEG image file. 👁 Look up *JPEG*.

jump list A *jump list* is a web page containing links to other web pages. 👁 Look up *hyperlink* and *web page*.

junk e-mail *Junk e-mail* is the electronic counterpart of paper junk mail. It is unsolicited electronic mail, usually in the form of advertisements. Often these advertisements are for products and/or businesses in which the recipient of the e-mail has no interest. Sometimes the advertisements are offensive. There is legislation before Congress to place heavy restrictions on junk e-mail.

junk fax A *junk fax* is an unsolicited advertisement sent by fax. Junk faxing is illegal in the United States.

justification *Justification* is how the beginnings and the endings of lines of text are aligned. 👁 Look up *left justified, ragged left, ragged right,* and *right justified.*

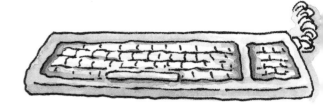

K (1) *K* is an abbreviation for kilobyte. A kilobyte is about 1,000 bytes. (It is exactly 1,024 bytes, which is equal to 2^{10}.) 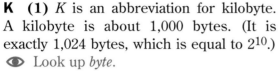 Look up *byte*.

(2) *K* is an abbreviation for "OK." It is used in informal e-mail, chat, and Usenet.

Noya: **k**. *If you don't want to play board games, then let's play hide and seek.*
Jana: **k**.

See the appendix, pages 189–190, for a complete table of abbreviations. Look up *chat, e-mail,* and *Usenet.*

kBps *kBps* is an abbreviation for **ki**lo**b**ytes **p**er **s**econd. It means that about 1,000 bytes of data are transmitted every second by a device. Look up *byte* and *data.*

kbps *kbps* is an abbreviation for kilobits per second. It means that about 1,000 bits of data are transmitted every second by a device. Look up *bit* and *data.*

keyboard A *keyboard* is what you use to type information into a computer. The keyboard is a plastic holder filled with keys (also called pads). The keys have letters, numbers, or other symbols on them. The keyboard is the most common way of interfacing with a computer. Keyboards for Macintosh computers are slightly different from keyboards for PCs. Both are shown on page 5. Look up *information, interface, keyboard, PC, Macintosh,* and *symbol.*

keyboard buffer The *keyboard buffer* is an area in memory that stores keystrokes until the program is ready to accept them. Look up *keystroke, memory,* and *program.*

keyboard cursor A *keyboard cursor* is a character that shows where the next character will appear. Keyboard cursors often flash on and off. Look up *character.*

keypress Look up *keystroke.*

keystroke A *keystroke* is the pressing of an individual key found on a keyboard. Look up *keyboard.*

kg *kg* is an abbreviation for kilogram. Look up *kilogram.*

kill To *kill* a program is to stop running it. To kill a file is to erase it from your computer's memory.

> *John decided to **kill** a file, so he erased all the data in the file. Later, he learned that his PC was automatically creating backup files, so the file wasn't really erased.*

👁 Look up *backup copy, file, memory, PC, program,* and *run.*

kilo- *kilo-* is a prefix than means 1,000. In computer and Internet usage, it means 1,024 (which equals 2^{10}). 👁 Look up *mega-, prefix,* and *tera-.*

kilobyte A *kilobyte* is about 1,000 bytes. (It is exactly 1,024 bytes, which equals 2^{10}.) 👁 Look up *byte.*

kilogram A *kilogram* is a metric measure of mass equal to 1,000 grams or 2.205 pounds.

kilometer A *kilometer* is a metric measure of length equal to 1,000 meters or 0.62 mile.

LAN *LAN* is an acronym for local-area network. 👁 Look up *local-area network*.

landscape orientation *Landscape orientation* is a computer display in which the image is longer from left to right than it is from top to bottom. 👁 Look up *image* and *portrait orientation*.

laptop computer A *laptop computer* is a computer that is small enough to fit onto a person's lap. A laptop computer is easy to carry and operates on batteries. Smaller laptop computers are called notebook computers or subnotebook computers depending on their size.

LaserJet *LaserJet* is a successful line of Hewlett-Packard printers. 👁 Look up *Hewlett-Packard*.

laser printer A *laser printer* is a printer that uses a laser beam and toner to create text and images on paper. 👁 Look up *image* and *text*.

launch **(1)** To *launch* a program is to start the program. 👁 Look up *program*.

(2) To *launch* a new product is to offer the new product for sale.

leader A *leader* is a line of dots connecting an item on one side of the page with an item on the opposite side. Leaders are often used in tables of contents.

left arrow key The *left arrow key* is the key on the keyboard that makes the cursor move to the left. 👁 Look up *cursor* and *keyboard.*

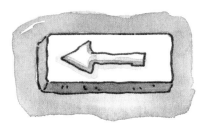

left-click When you click with the left mouse button, you are performing a *left-click.* 👁 Look up *right-click.*

left justified A *left justified* block of text is aligned on the left side.

    Is all text left justified? No. Situations occur in which text is not left justified. Subordinate items in an outline are not usually left justified. Some poems use the shape of the poem on the page for a special effect and may not be left justified. Text in web pages may not be left justified if the web page designer wants to achieve a special effect. 👁 Look up *text, web design,* and *web page.*

legal size Paper used for legal documents in the United States is 8½ × 14 inches, or *legal size.* 👁 Look up *letter size.*

letter size Paper used for business correspondence in the United States is 8½ × 11 inches, or *letter size.* 👁 Look up *legal size.*

letterspacing The space between letters is called *letterspacing.*

line spacing The spacing between lines of type is known as *line spacing.* Most word processor allow the user to set the line spacing. Teachers often require students to double space papers. Double spacing is easier to read and provides more room between lines for marking corrections and comments. 👁 Look up *word processor.*

line surge A *line surge* happens when a large amount of current suddenly passes through the electric lines to your computer.

Can a line surge damage my computer? Yes. Line surges are a serious problem for computers.

How can I protect my computer from a line surge? You can buy devices to help protect your computer from a line surge. These devices are called surge protectors.  Look up *device* and *surge protector.*

link 👁 Look up *hyperlink.*

Linux *Linux* is an operating system for PCs and other computers that is used with UNIX. Many Internet service providers, businesses, and universities use Linux, and it is popular among professional programmers. Linux is distributed freely (subject to conditions). 👁 Look up *Internet service provider, operating system, PC, programmer,* and *UNIX.*

load To *load* a file is to transfer a file from a disk to memory so that the computer can use it. 👁 Look up *disk, file,* and *memory.*

local-area network A *local-area network* is a special type of network that connects users who are near each other, usually in the same building. Larger networks are called wide-area networks (WANs). Smaller networks (for example, two or three connected computers in the same room) are called tiny-area networks (TANs). The Internet is a set of connected WANs. ◉ Look up *acronym, network, tiny-area network,* and *wide-area network.*

LocalTalk A *LocalTalk* connection allows a Macintosh computer to connect to an Appletalk Network. ◉ Look up *computer, Macintosh,* and *network.*

lock up To *lock up* means to stop accepting input. A locked up computer is frozen and will do nothing, no matter what keys you press. The user must reboot the computer.

Does rebooting the computer always solve the problem? Not always. Sometimes the problem is serious enough that you will have to have an expert repair your computer. ◉ Look up *reboot.*

log off To *log off* is to turn off any computer activities and to indicate to the computer system that you will stop using the computer. ◉ Look up *computer.*

log on To *log on* is to indicate to a computer system that you will begin using the computer. On some computer systems, you must enter your name and a special

password before the computer will work. ◉ Look up *password.*

log in ◉ Look up *log on.*

LOL *LOL* is an abbreviation for "laughing out loud." It is used in informal e-mail, chat, and Usenet.

> *Mary: I'm **lol**.*
> *Paul: Why?*
> *Mary: My big brother, the "game wizard" just got a new board game, and I beat him three times already.*
> *Paul: Wow! Congrats.*

See the appendix, pages 189–190, for a complete table of abbreviations. ◉ Look up *chat, e-mail,* and *Usenet.*

long sentence A *long sentence* is a name that grammar-checking programs give to sentences that are too long for the grammar checker to analyze. Such sentences are not always incorrect. Still, checking and revising long sentences is a good idea.

....

lossless compression *Lossless compression* is compression of a file without loss of information. For example, GIF is a lossless compression method. 👁 Look up *data compression, file, information, GIF,* and *lossy compression.*

....

lossy compression *Lossy compression* is compression of a file with possible loss of information. For example, JPEG is a lossy compression method. 👁 Look up *data compression, file, information, GIF,* and *lossless compression.*

....

lowercase The *lowercase* letters are *a, b, c, d, e, f, g, h, i, j, k, l, m, n, o, p, q, r, s, t, u, v, w, x, y,* and *z.* 👁 Look up *case insensitive* and *case sensitive.*

....

LPT The DOS operating system recognizes the parallel printer ports by the letters *LPT.* The first parallel port is LPT1, the second is LPT2, and so on. 👁 Look up *operating system, port,* and *printer.*

....

ls *ls* is a UNIX command that instructs the computer to show the contents of a directory. 👁 Look up *command, directory,* and *UNIX.*

....

LTNS *LTNS* is an abbreviation for "long time no see." It is used in informal e-mail, chat, and Usenet.

> *John:* **ltns.** *You haven't been online for weeks. What happened?*
> *Juan: I've been in London for two months visiting my grandmother.*

See the appendix, pages 189–190, for a complete table of abbreviations. 👁 Look up *chat, e-mail,* and *Usenet.*

....

M *M* stands for mega. When you see mega before a word, it means to multiply by one million (1,000,000). For example, a megabyte is about 1,000,000 bytes. (It is exactly 1,048,576 bytes, which equals 2^{20} bytes.) 👁 Look up *byte*.

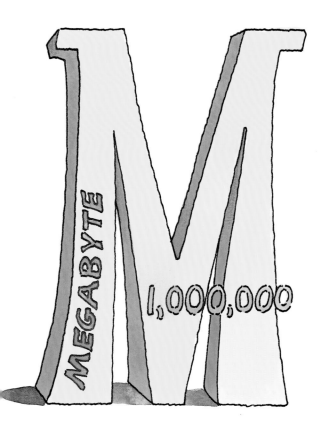

Mac *Mac* means Macintosh, a computer made by Apple Computer, Incorporated

and introduced in 1984. 👁 Look up *computer* and *Macintosh*.

Mac clone A *Mac clone* is a clone of a Macintosh computer. A Mac clone is made to run all of the same software and to do the same things that a Macintosh computer does. 👁 Look up *Apple Computer, Incorporated; clone;* and *Macintosh*.

Mac OS *Mac OS* is the formal name of the Macintosh operating system. 👁 Look up *Macintosh* and *operating system*.

machine A *machine* is a mechanical thing that does something. Machines usually have many parts and are often electric. A computer is a machine and so is an automobile and a typewriter.

machine-dependent program A program that works on only one type of computer is said to be a *machine dependent program.*  Look up *program.*

machine-independent program A program that works on many types of computers is said to be a *machine independent program.* Look up *program.*

machine language *Machine language* is the language that the CPU of a computer uses. It is a set of numbers, each of which instructs the CPU to do some particular thing. Look up *CPU.*

Macintosh The *Macintosh* is a computer made by Apple Computer, Incorporated. It was introduced in 1984 and was the first personal computer to have a graphical user interface (GUI). The Macintosh, in all its versions, has been a major force in personal computing. Look up *Apple Computers, Incorporated; iBook; iMac; graphical user interface,* and *Macintosh.*

mailbox A *mailbox* is the space in an e-mail system where your e-mail messages are deposited.

(2) A *malfunction* is an error or a breakdown, such as when a computer does something that it is not supposed to do.

mainframe A *mainframe* is a large computer that can be used by many people at the same time. Mainframe computers are usually too large to move easily. Today's desktop computers, or even laptop computers, have more computing power than the mainframes of just a few decades ago. 👁 Look up *desktop computer* and *laptop computer.*

malfunction **(1)** To *malfunction* is to stop working correctly.

management information systems (MIS) *Management information systems* is the study of efficient systems for developing and making use of information within an organization. People are included as part of the complete information system. 👁 Look up *information.*

marquee Some web pages have scrolling messages with text or images moving across the screen. A scrolling message such as this is called a *marquee*. For example, a marquee may look like this:

and then this:

> (-:

and then this:

> lo!!! (-:

and then this:

> :-) Hello!!! (-:

and then this:

> :-) Hel

and then this:

> :-)

Finally, the message may begin again:

> (-:

and repeat.

👁 Look up *image, scroll, text, web design, web page,* and *World Wide Web.*

---

maximize   To *maximize* is to make a window fill the whole screen or to become as large as possible. To maximize a window on a PC, click the mouse on the maximize button in the right-hand corner. On a Macintosh, use the zoom box on the far right side of the title bar to maximize a window. 👁 Look up *Macintosh, minimize mouse, PC, screen,* and *window.*

MB   *MB* is an abbreviation for megabyte. A megabyte is about one million (1,000,000) bytes. (It is exactly 1,048,576 bytes.) 👁 Look up *byte.*

MBps   *MBps* is an abbreviation for **m**ega**b**ytes **p**er **s**econd. The number of MBps is the number of megabytes of information transmitted per second by a device. 👁 Look up *byte* and *information.*

Mbps   *Mbps* is an abbreviation for **m**ega**b**its **p**er **s**econd. The number of Mbps is the number of megabits of information transmitted per second by a device. 👁 Look up *bit.*

---

mega-   *mega-* is a prefix meaning one million (1,000,000). In computer and Internet usage, it means 1,048,576 (which equals 2^{20}). 👁 Look up *Internet, kilo-, prefix,* and *tera-.*

---

megabyte   A *megabyte* is about one million (1,000,000) bytes. (It is exactly 1,048,576 bytes, which is 2^{20} bytes.) 👁 Look up *byte.*

---

megahertz (MHz)   A *megahertz* is 1,000,000 hertz. Since a hertz (Hz) is one cycle, a megahertz is 1,000,000 cycles. The speed of a computer is measured in megahertz. 👁 Look up *Hz.*

---

memory   *Memory* is the place where your computer stores information that it is currently using. There are different kinds of memory. RAM means random-access memory. Your computer can read and write to RAM. ROM means read-only memory. Your computer can only read from ROM, but cannot write to ROM. Information can be retrieved much faster from memory than from a disk. 👁 Look up *disk, information, RAM, ROM,* and *retrieve.*

menu A *menu* is a list of items from which you select things to tell a computer to do. When you use computers and the Internet, you will see many menus. You select an item from a menu by clicking on it with your mouse or by using the arrow keys and

pressing enter. 👁 Look up *arrow keys, column, Internet,* and *symbols.*

menu bar A *menu bar* is a narrow rectangular area on which a choice of menus appears.

> *"Dad, I want to check the spelling in my letter," Tom said.*
> *"Just click Tools on the **menu bar** and then click Spelling and Grammar, son," Tom's father said.*

👁 Look up *menu.*

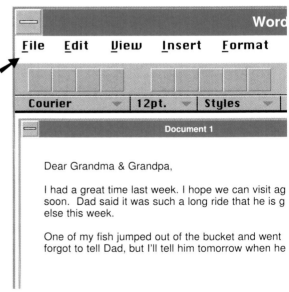

menu item A *menu item* is part of a menu. Each menu item tells the computer to do something or, on web sites, lists something you can see or do on the site. 👁 Look up *menu* and *web site.*

message A *message* is any kind of communication. You can send and receive messages by e-mail, for example. Also, your computer sometimes gives you messages about what it is doing or is about to do. 👁 Look up *communicate* and *e-mail*.

message box A *message box* is a small window that gives the user information. For example, the box can question whether you want to save a document before closing it or tell you that a document did not print. The box will usually disappear when the user clicks on the mouse button. 👁 Look up *alert box* and *window*.

meter A *meter* is the metric unit of length. One meter equals 3.281 feet or 39.37 inches.

MHz 👁 Look up *Hz*.

microchip 👁 Look up *integrated circuit*.

microprocessor The *microprocessor* of a computer is a chip that contains the CPU (central processing unit). All of the most important operations your computer performs happen in the microprocessor. 👁 Look up *CPU*.

Microsoft Corporation *Microsoft Corporation* is a leader in the computer software business. Microsoft made MS-DOS, the first PC-operating system, and makes Windows. Microsoft also makes Microsoft Word and Microsoft Internet Explorer. 👁 Look up *Microsoft Internet Explorer, MS-DOS, PC, software,* and *Windows*.

Microsoft Internet Explorer *Microsoft Internet Explorer* is a popular web browser made by Microsoft. 👁 Look up *browser*.

Microsoft Windows *Microsoft Windows* is an operating system for IBM PC computers and PC clones. It is the most popular operating system for PCs. It features a graphical user interface (GUI, pronounced G—U—I or "gooey"). A graphical user interface lets users control the computer by moving a pointer using a mouse, a trackball, or some other pointing device and clicking on icons to perform operations. 👁 Look up *clone, graphical user interface, icon, mouse, operating system, PC, pointing device, trackball,* and *user*.

milli- *milli-* is a prefix than means one-thousandth (1/1,000). 👁 Look up *prefix*.

millimeter A *millimeter* is a small length equal to one-thousandth (1/1,000) of a meter. The lead in a standard pencil, for example, is about 1 millimeter wide.

millisecond A *millisecond* is a small period of time equal to one-thousandth (1/1,000) of a second. Milliseconds can be used to measure how long memory devices, such as hard disks or CD-ROMs, take to access information. 👁 Look up *access, access time, device, hard drive,* and *memory.*

minicomputer A *minicomputer* is a computer that is smaller than a mainframe but larger than a desktop computer. 👁 Look up *desktop computer* and *mainframe.*

minimize To *minimize* is to make a window as small as possible. To minimize a window, click the mouse on the minimize button. 👁 Look up *maximize, mouse,* and *window.*

MIPS *MIPS* is an abbreviation for **m**illion **i**nstructions **p**er **s**econd. The measure of MIPS gives an idea of how fast a computer operates.

mirror site A *mirror site* is a web site that has the same content as another web site but is located in another, separate, location.

> *"John, have you seen the new web site about the next week's football game?"*
>
> *"I tried, but too many people were accessing the site."*
>
> *"Use the **mirror site** then. It has the same information. I'll get the address for you."*

👁 Look up *web site.*

MIS 👁 Look up *management information systems.*

mixed case *Mixed case* is type set with regular capitalization.

mkdir *mkdir* is a UNIX command that instructs the computer to create a new directory. 👁 Look up *command, directory,* and *UNIX.*

mm *mm* is an abbreviation for millimeter. A millimeter is a small length equal to one-thousandth (1/1,000) of a meter. 👁 Look up *meter.*

modem A *modem* is a device that lets your computer communicate with other computers over phone lines. Some modems are housed in small boxes. Others are cards

that are installed inside your computer. 👁 Look up *card, communicate,* and *device.*

modifier key A *modifier key* is a key that is pressed at the same time as another key to give the second key a different meaning. The new meaning depends on the program you are using. In many applications, you can program a meaning of your choice for the modifier key. For example, you may program the combination [Alt] [D] to make a degree symbol, °. 👁 Look up *program.*

monitor (1) A *monitor* is the part of a computer system that looks like a television and displays information when you use the computer. The monitor does not compute, and it does not store any data. It only displays information.

(2) A *monitor* is a program that controls what other programs can do. 👁 Look up *data, information,* and *program.*

monitor resolution *Monitor resolution* is a measure of the number of pixels that your computer's monitor displays. The higher the resolution, the sharper the image is on the screen. 👁 Look up *image, monitor,* and *resolution.*

monochrome *Monochrome* means one color. A monochrome monitor can only display only one color plus the background color. 👁 Look up *monitor.*

mono-spaced font A *mono-spaced font* is a font whose characters take up exactly the same amount of space, as contrasted with proportionally spaced fonts. For example, Courier is a mono-spaced font, and Times New Roman is a proportionally spaced font. Here is the same greeting in Courier and in Times New Roman:

Courier:
```
        Hello, Milo!
```

Times New Roman:
    Hello, Milo!

Notice that, with Courier, the space taken up by the letters is the same for each letter. With Times New Roman, the *l*s, for example, take up less space than the H. 👁 Look up *character* and *proportionally spaced font.*

morph To *morph* is to change one thing into something else. Many graphics programs use morphing. For example, in a video game, you may see a human turn into an animal. 👁 Look up *program.*

motherboard Inside your computer are many boards with wire, chips, and a lot of electronic components. The most important board is the *motherboard.* The CPU and primary memory are on the motherboard. All other boards, disk drives, and peripherals are connected to the motherboard. 👁 Look up *disk drive, integrated circuit,* and *peripheral.*

motion blur *Motion blur* is a feature offered in certain paint and 3-D programs that blurs an image to give it the illusion of motion.

Motorola *Motorola* is a leading manufacturer of electronic equipment and microprocessors. It can be found on the web at *http://www.mot.com.* 👁 Look up *micro-processor.*

mount   To *mount* is to add a device to a computer. 👁 Look up *device.*

mouse   A *mouse* is a small box with buttons that you move around to control things on your computer screen. Often the mouse controls a pointer, which appears on the screen. The pointer is usually displayed as an arrow. 👁 Look up *mouse, mouse pointer,* and *screen.*

mouse button   A *mouse button* is a button on a mouse. You press the button to cause the pointer to select an object on the screen or to cause your computer to take some other action. 👁 Look up *mouse* and *mouse pointer.*

mouse cursor   👁 Look up *mouse pointer.*

mouse driven   A software program is *mouse driven* if you control it by using a mouse. 👁 Look up *mouse* and *software program.*

mouse pad   A *mouse pad* is a mat on which your mouse sits as you move it around. Mouse pads can be made of fabric or plastic. Some have pictures. 👁 Look up *mouse.*

mouse pointer   A *mouse pointer* is an object on your computer screen that you move with your mouse, trackball, or some other pointing device to select items. The mouse pointer is usually an arrow, but the image can be anything from a magician's wand to a frog. Many programs have mouse pointers meant for the particular type of program. For example, the mouse pointer of an art program may be an artist's paintbrush. 👁 Look up *computer screen, mouse, pointing device, program,* and *trackball.*

mouse support If a software program has *mouse support,* then you can use your mouse (or other pointer device) to operate the software program. 👁 Look up *mouse, program,* and *software.*

movie length *Movie length* is the amount of time that a video clip takes to play. 👁 Look up *video clip.*

.mov The suffix *.mov* means that a file is a QuickTime movie. 👁 Look up *QuickTime* and *suffix.*

MP3 *MP3* is an abbreviation for MPEG-I Audio Layer III. MP3 is a format for recording and playing music. MP3 files are music files, and they can be played like a CD or a cassette recording. 👁 Look up *file.*

MPC *MPC* is the abbreviation for **m**ulti-media **p**ersonal **c**omputer. An MPC is a personal computer that meets the specific requirements for compact disc, sound, and graphics capacities. These requirements are established by the MPC Marketing Council and are frequently revised. 👁 Look up *compact disc* and *graphics.*

MPEG (pronounced "m-peg") *MPEG* stands for **M**otion **P**icture **E**xperts **G**roup. MPEG is a format for movie files. When you play MPEG files, you see a movie on your screen. 👁 Look up *file, format,* and *screen.*

.mpg The suffix *.mpg* means that a file is an MPEG movie. 👁 Look up *MPEG* and *suffix.*

MRU *MRU* is the abbreviation for "most recently used."

MRU list An *MRU list* is a list of a user's most recently used files or web addresses. Many word processor and web browsers keep MRU lists so the user can quickly return to a document or site. 👁 Look up *file, site,* and *web address.*

MS *MS* is an abbreviation for Microsoft System.

ms *ms* is an abbreviation for millisecond. A millisecond is one one-thousandth (1/1,000) of a second. Computers do things is milliseconds. 👁 Look up *computer.*

MS-DOS *MS-DOS* is an acronym for **M**icro**s**oft **d**isk **o**perating **s**ystem. MS-DOS is the operating system used on most IBM and IBM-compatible computers. 👁 Look up *acronym, IBM, Microsoft Corporation,* and *operating system.*

MSN *MSN* is the abbreviation for **M**icro**s**oft **N**etwork. MSN is a network founded by Microsoft that provides content as well as access to the Internet. 👁 Look up *access provider, content provider,* and *Internet.*

multimedia A *multimedia* presentation is a presentation of information on a computer that uses text, pictures, sound, and possibly interactive routines. Multimedia is an important use of computers. You can find entertaining and educational multimedia about topics ranging from the history of China to mathematics. 👁 Look up *information, interactive,* and *text.*

multiprocessing If a computer has multiple CPUs that collaborate in the execution of a program, then it is *multiprocessing.* 👁 Look up *CPU* and *program.*

multitasking A task is a job. The prefix multi- means many. *Multitasking* means doing many jobs. Multitasking would be like juggling, eating, painting a wall, and grooming your dog all at the same time! Today, the computers that most people use are capable of multitasking. For example, unless you are using an older computer, your computer can probably run a word processor and a video game at the same time. 👁 Look up *word processor.*

multi user *Multi user* means more than one user. A multi user computer is a computer that can be used by more than one person at the same time.

My Computer The *My Computer* folder is a special folder on computers running the Windows 95 and Windows 98 operating systems. It contains icons for disk drives and system folders.

nanosecond A *nanosecond* is one-billionth (1/1,000,000,000) of a second. Computers can do some things in nanoseconds.

natural language A *natural language* is any human language, such as English, French, Chinese, Greek, or pig Latin. Computers do not use natural languages. They use machine language. Programmers use programming languages such as BASIC, Pascal, and C++, which can be translated or compiled into machine language instructions. Many programmers are trying to make computers understand natural language. They have had some success. However, it is a difficult task because the natural languages that you and all humans speak are very complicated. 👁 Look up *BASIC, C++, machine language,* and *programming language.*

navigation The act of moving around a system of menus, help files, or the web. Finding your way around can sometimes be confusing, especially on the web. If you think you will want to return to a particular web page, bookmark it or add it to your Favorites folder. 👁 Look up *bookmark, Favorites folder, menu,* and *World Wide Web.*

net *net* is a top-level Internet domain name that indicates a network. 👁 Look up *com, edu, gov,* and *org.*

Net, the 👁 Look up *Internet.*

netiquette (short for **net**work **etiquette**) When using the Internet, be polite and have respect for other users. All the things that you should do to be polite and to show such respect are called *netiquette.* For example, do not be rude in chat rooms and do not send people e-mail that they probably will

not want. There are many other rules. 👁 Look up *e-mail, Internet,* and *Chat.*

---

netizen (short for Inter**net** cit**izen**) The people in your neighborhood make up a community. The people who use the Internet also make up a community. A *netizen* is a person who uses the Internet and is therefore a member of the Internet community. So, if you use the Internet, especially a lot, then you are a netizen. 👁 Look up *Internet.*

Netscape Navigator *Netscape Navigator* is a web browser produced by Netscape Communications Corporation. AOL, an Internet access provider, acquired Netscape in 1998. 👁 Look up *access provider, AOL, browser, Internet,* and *World Wide Web.*

---

network When two or more computers are able to communicate with one another, you have a network. *Networks* come in many sizes, from two or three computers connected in the same room (a tiny-area network or TAN) to the Internet, which links computers all over the world. 👁 Look up *Internet, local-area network, tiny-area network,* and *wide-area network.*

Network Solutions, Inc. Until 1998, *Network Solutions, Inc.* was solely responsible for the registration of top-level domain names ending in .com, .net, and .org, under a contract with the U.S. government. Since 1998, Network Solutions competes with several domain name registrars. Network Solutions can be found on the web at *www.networksolutions.com.* 👁 Look up *com, net,* and *org.*

---

newbie *Newbie* is a nickname for a newcomer to the Internet, a newsgroup, or other computer network group. 👁 Look up *Internet* and *newsgroup.*

---

newsgroup A *newsgroup* is a discussion area on a computer network. Users can post messages and read all posted messages. Usenet is a popular distributor of newsgroups. 👁 Look up *network* and *Usenet.*

---

newspaper columns If you are using a word processor and you want to make a document that looks like a newspaper, you can use the *newspaper columns* format. Newspaper column format arranges text in columns, just like in a newspaper or magazine. 👁 Look up *text* and *word processor.*

---

nibble Four bits make a *nibble.* A nibble is one-half of a byte. 👁 Look up *bit* and *byte.*

NIC *NIC* is the abbreviation for **N**etwork **I**nterface **C**ard. An NIC is a circuit board inserted inside a computer that enables it to connect to a local-area network. 👁 Look up *circuit board* and *local-area network.*

Nom *Nom* is a suffix indicating that an e-mail address or web site is a personal site. 👁 Look up *com, net, org,* and *web site.*

---

non-system disk error You will see the *non-system disk error* message when you turn on your computer for two common reasons. First, a diskette may be in drive A. If it is, remove it and press enter. Another possibility is a serious hard drive problem. If turning the computer off and then back on does not solve the problem, you need a repair specialist. The actual non-system disk error message is:

Non-system disk or disk error
Replace and press any key when ready

👁 Look up *diskette* and *hard drive.*

---

notebook computer A *notebook computer* is a small laptop computer. Notebook computers are usually small enough to fit into a briefcase or backpack. 👁 Look up *laptop computer.*

NotePad *NotePad* is a text editor for Windows. 👁 Look up *text editor* and *Windows.*

NP *NP* is the abbreviation for "no problem." It is used in informal e-mail, chat, and Usenet.

> *Mike: My car is back in the shop again. Now I have no way to get to work tomorrow.*
> *Sara: I'll give you a ride. What time do you have to be there.*
> *Mike: I start at 10. Are you sure you don't mind?*
> *Sara:* **np.** *I start work at 10:15 and it's right around the corner.*

See the appendix, pages 189–190, for a complete table of abbreviations. 👁 Look up *chat, e-mail,* and *Usenet.*

---

ns *ns* is an abbreviation for nanosecond. 👁 Look up *nanosecond.*

NuBus A *NuBus* is an expansion bus that is usually found on older Macintosh computers. To interface with a NuBus computer card, your computer must have a NuBus expansion slot. 👁 Look up *bus, expansion slot,* and *interface.*

Num Lock key The *Num Lock key* is a key on your keyboard. It acts as a toggle switch, putting the numeric keypad into numeric or cursor control mode. In numeric mode, you can use the numeric keyboard to enter numbers. In cursor control mode, you can use the numeric keyboard to move the cursor around the screen. 👁 Look up *cursor, keyboard, numeric keypad, screen,* and *toggle.*

numeric keypad The *numeric keypad* is a set of number keys arranged in adding-machine order. It is on the right side of most keyboards. The keypad can be used to enter numbers or as a cursor control, depending on the Num Lock key setting.

Entering numbers using the numeric keypad is often easier than using the number keys at the top of your keyboard, especially when you are entering a lot of numbers. 👁 Look up *cursor, keyboard,* and *Num Lock key.*

numerical order To arrange the items in a list in *numerical order* is to arrange the items with the smallest number first, the greatest number last, and the other numbers arranged so that each subsequent one is larger than the previous number.

object-oriented images *Object-oriented images* display items by representing them as a system of geometric lines instead of by using dots. 👁 Look up *image* and *resolution.*

OBO *OBO* is an abbreviation for "or best offer." It is used in informal e-mail, chat, and Usenet.

> For sale. Baseball cards—the best of 1999 (Yankees) $100 **obo**.

See the appendix, pages 189–190, for a complete table of abbreviations. 👁 Look up *chat, e-mail,* and *Usenet.*

*"It's an old computer, Son. It's slow and doesn't run the newer software, so it is **obsolete** now. Mr. Johnson has bought a newer and better computer."*

obsolete Something is *obsolete* if it is no longer used by most people. For example, rotary telephones are obsolete, and you probably would not see one being used except in an old movie.

You will hear the word obsolete often when you use computers and the Internet because computer equipment and programs become outdated fast. Computers that were state-of-the-art five or ten years ago are usually considered completely obsolete now.

> *"Dad, why does Mr. Johnson use that computer as a doorstop?"*

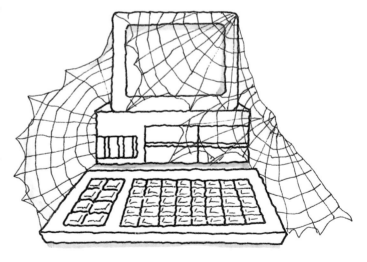

👁 Look up *Internet* and *program.*

123

OCR *OCR* is an abbreviation for **o**ptical **c**haracter **r**ecognition. OCR lets a computer scan a typed page and input the text into a word processor file for you to use.  Look up *optical character reader, text,* and *word processor.*

---

off-line (1) To be *off-line* is to be unable to work. A machine can be off-line for many different reasons, perhaps because of a loss of power, a mechanical defect, or an operating bug.

(2) If you have Internet service but are not using it, then you are *off-line*. If you are part of a computer network but are not logged on, you are off-line. ◉ Look up *bug, Internet, log on,* and *network.*

OIC *OIC* is an abbreviation for "oh, I see." It is used in informal e-mail, chat, and Usenet.

> *John: Why didn't you show up today at the mall like we talked about?*
> *Juan: I did go to the mall at 6 P.M. in front of the theater, but you weren't there.*
> *John: **oic**, I was waiting at the food court next to the theater. Sorry.*

See the appendix, pages 189–190, for a complete table of abbreviations. ◉ Look up *chat, e-mail,* and *Usenet.*

OMG *OMG* is the abbreviation for **O**bject **M**anagement **G**roup. OMG is an association of hundreds of computer companies that work on standards for software

components to interact with each other. You can find OMG on the web at *http://www.omg.org.* ◉ Look up *software.*

---

on-board *On-board* is an expression meaning that something is included within a piece of equipment. For example, sound cards often have on-board amplifiers, so an outside amplifier is not needed. ◉ Look up *sound card.*

---

online (1) When you are connected to a network, you are *online*.

(2) Something that is on a computer network is *online*. For example, if you want information about a new model airplane, the company that makes the model airplane may have online information available. If so, you can connect to the Internet to learn about the model airplane by visiting the company's web site.

(3) When a computer accessory like a printer or scanner is connected to your computer and ready to use, it is *online*.  Look up *Internet, network, printer,* and *scanner.*

online help If you are using a computer and find something that you cannot do, you can often get *online help*. You get the help by using your mouse to click help or by typing a command. When you ask for it, help will appear as a menu of answers to your problem.  Look up *click, menu,* and *mouse.*

online service *Online service* is a telephone or cable connection that connects your computer to other computers that are connected to an online system. Online service lets you use e-mail, the Internet, and other computer-to-computer activities. Online services usually charge a fee for what they help you to do.  Look up *e-mail, Internet,* and *Internet service provider.*

online trading The act of buying or selling stocks or securities through the Internet is known as *online trading*. The brokerage fees are lower and the transactions are completed more quickly.  Look up *Internet.*

open To *open* a file or document is to call it from its storage location (for example, a disk) and bring it to the screen so that you can work with it.  Look up *document* and *file.*

operating system An *operating system* is a program that performs a computer's basic tasks such as running commands, overseeing files and directories, and operating peripheral devices such as printers. The operating system is the most important program in a computer. It is like a ship's captain and commanders, each directing a different task.  Look up *device, directory, file, peripheral,* and *printer.*

Operating System/2 👁 Look up *OS/2*.

optical character reader An *optical character reader* is a device that reads words from a page and inputs them into a computer. Some optical character readers are built into copy machines, and some are handheld. 👁 Look up *device* and *scanner*.

optical character recognition *Optical character recognition* is done by optical character readers. Often written as OCR, optical character recognition is the way that words are moved from a page of paper into a computer while allowing the words in the computer to be changed by editing. 👁 Look up *edit* and *optical character reader*.

optical disk An *optical disk* is a storage device. The information is stored through the process of a laser etching tiny grooves in the plastic disk. 👁 Look up *CD-ROM, disk,* and *information*.

optical mouse An *optical mouse* is a type of mouse that uses light reflected from a special mouse pad, instead of a ball, to control the mouse pointer. A beam of light shines from the bottom of the mouse and is reflected by the mouse pad back to the mouse. Electronics inside the mouse then use the reflected light to direct movement of the mouse pointer on your computer screen. 👁 Look up *mouse, mouse pointer,* and *mouse pad*.

optical scanner 👁 Look up *scanner*.

optimizer An *optimizer* is a program that organizes files so that the user can find programs more easily. 👁 Look up *file* and *program*.

option key The *option key* is a modifier key on Macintosh keyboards that can help give special commands to your computer. To give a special command, you press the option key and at least one other key at the same time. On other computers, the Alt key works as the option key. 👁 Look up *Alt key, command, keyboard,* and *modifier key*.

Oracle *Oracle* is a corporation that produces software. It can be located on the web at *http://www.oracle.com*.

org *org* is a top-level Internet domain name that indicates a nonprofit organization. 👁 Look up *com, edu, gov,* and *net.*

orientation In printing and word processing, an image can have one of two orientations. Landscape *orientation* means that the page is longer from left to right than it is from top to bottom. Portrait *orientation* means that the page is longer from top to bottom that from left to right. When you print a document, you can usually choose which orientation you want. 👁 Look up *image, landscape orientation, portrait orientation,* and *word processing.*

PORTRAIT

LANDSCAPE

orphan   Good form says that at least two lines of a paragraph should be on any page, never only one line. An *orphan* is the first line of a paragraph when that line appears by itself at the bottom of a page. Many word processors are programmed to eliminate orphans automatically. 👁 Look up *program, widow,* and *word processor.*

．．

OS/2   *OS/2* is an operating system that can run DOS and Windows programs and allows multitasking. OS/2 competes with Microsoft Windows and UNIX. Overall, most computer users do not use OS/2. 👁 Look up *DOS, multitasking, operating system, program, UNIX,* and *Windows.*

．．

OTOH   *OTOH* is the abbreviation for "on the other hand." It is used in informal e-mail, chat, and Usenet.

Allan: I really have to finish mowing the lawn.
Keith: Well, that's too bad because we are going to beach. Then we're going to have a barbeque.
Allan: **otoh***, the lawn will still need mowing tomorrow. What time are we leaving for the beach?*

See the appendix on pages 189–190, for a complete table of abbreviations. 👁 Look up *chat, e-mail,* and *Usenet.*

．．

output   Any image, text, or result of a calculation that comes from a computer is *output.* 👁 Look up *image* and *text.*

．．

output device   Any device that displays information of any kind from a computer is an *output device.* Monitors and printers are examples of output devices. 👁 Look up *device, information, monitor,* and *printer.*

．．

padlock icon The *padlock icon* on Netscape Navigator is a small icon that tells you whether the web site that you are viewing is secure or not. When the padlock is locked, the site is secure. If the padlock is unlocked, the site is not secure. 👁 Look up *icon, window,* and *web site.*

page down key The *page down key* is a key on your keyboard that moves the cursor to the previous page of the document. 👁 Look up *cursor, keyboard,* and *page up key.*

page up key The *page up key* is a key on your keyboard that moves the cursor to the

following page of the document. 👁 Look up *cursor, keyboard,* and *page down key.*

pages per minute When you use a printer, it may print fast or it may print slowly. *Pages per minute* is the number of pages of text a printer will print in a minute. 👁 Look up *printer* and *text.*

paint program A *paint program* is a system that lets you make color images by choosing the color of the dots used. 👁 Look up *image* and *pixel.*

palette (1) A *palette* is a set of specific colors.

(2) A *palette* is part of a graphics file that specifies the colors used in the file. 👁 Look up *file.*

Palm Pilot *Palm Pilot* is a series of hand-held computers made by Palm Computing, Inc. The newest version includes wireless Internet access. Palm Computing can be found on the web at *www.palm.com.*  Look up *Internet.*

parallel port A *parallel port* is a type of port. With a parallel port, data is transmitted several bits at a time. Printers are often connected to a parallel port of a computer. Look up *bit, data, port, printer,* and *serial port.*

parallel processing A computer capable of *parallel processing* can run different parts of a program at the same time. This makes computing faster. Look up *computer* and *program.*

park To *park* a disk drive means to set the mechanical parts so that they are safe.

They will not move around out of control and damage the disk. Parking a car keeps it from moving around out of control. Most computers do this automatically when they are shut down. Look up *disk* and *disk drive.*

Pascal *Pascal* is a programming language. Pascal is easy to learn and use. Like BASIC, it has easily recognizable code words. Look up *BASIC* and *programming language.*

passive voice A sentence is in the *passive voice* when its subject is acted upon. For example, "The ball was hit by John," is in the passive voice. In contrast, "John hit the ball," is in the active voice. Avoiding the passive voice when you are writing is usually best.

password Sometimes you have to enter a group of letters and/or symbols to start a computer, to access a web page, or to begin some other task on a computer. The group of letters and/or symbols is a *password.*

Here are some tips for protecting your password:

1. You should keep your password secret.

2. Do not use a word that could be found in a dictionary, because someone may use a program that can try all of the words in the dictionary. This will let that person discover your password and use it to do things that you may not want him or her to.

PATH In UNIX, DOS, and Windows, the operating system looks for files in the (working) directory. If the files are not there, the operating system has to look for the files in a specific list of directories. This specific list of directories is the *PATH*, like the path on a map. 👁 Look up *DOS, directory, operating system, UNIX,* and *Windows.*

3. Do not use obvious passwords, such as your name or the name of someone you know.

4. Add symbols if you use a real word. For example, add 123 if you use COW as a password, so the password will be COW123 or 123COW.

5. Change your password often.

👁 Look up *symbol* and *web page.*

paste *Paste* is an option that allows you to move material from a holding area into the document you are editing. 👁 Look up *cut* and *document.*

patch To *patch* a faulty piece of software means to change one or more of the software's files rather than to install an entire corrected copy. 👁 Look up *software.*

PC *PC* stands for **p**ersonal **c**omputer. However, when people say PC, they almost always mean an IBM personal computer or an IBM personal computer clone. 👁 Look up *computer* and *IBM.*

PC-DOS *PC-DOS* is the name that IBM gives to its PCs that use the IBM version of the DOS operating system. 👁 Look up *DOS, IBM,* and *PC.*

Pentium computer A *Pentium computer* is a computer that uses a Pentium,

Pentium II, or Pentium III microprocessor. 👁 Look up *computer* and *microprocessor.*

perforations *Perforations* are small holes in sheets of paper. For example, tractor-fed printers use paper with connected sheets. Perforations allow you to separate the sheets and to separate the tractor feed strips along the sides of the sheets. 👁 Look up *printer* and *tractor feed.*

perfs 👁 Look up *perforations.*

peripheral You can connect devices to a computer to allow it to do useful things. Any device like this, which adds a feature to a computer but is not necessary for the computer to work, is called a *peripheral.* Examples of peripherals include printers, disk drives, CD-ROM drives, Zip drives, sound boards, and modems. 👁 Look up *CD-ROM player, device, disk drive, modem, printer,* and *Zip drive.*

perl *Perl* is an abbreviation for **P**ractical **E**xtraction and **R**eport **L**anguage. Perl is a programming language used for looking at text files, extracting information from those files, and summarizing this information. 👁 Look up *file, information,* and *text.*

personal computer A *personal computer* is a small, self-contained computer system meant for individual use at home or in an office. Word processing, accounting, playing games, and surfing the Internet are common uses of personal computers. 👁 Look up *computer.*

PgDn key 👁 Look up *page down key.*

PgUp key 👁 Look up *page up key.*

Photo CD *Photo CD* is Eastman Kodak Company's system for storing images in digital form and displaying the same images on a high-resolution screen. The process used is secret.

pica A pica is a unit of measurement equal to about 1/6 of an inch or 12 points. Points are used in printing. 👁 Look up *point.*

pie chart A *pie chart* is a graph that is round like a pie. It shows how much of the

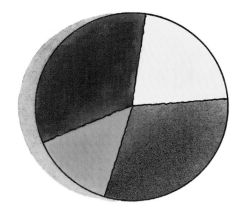

whole different values are. Each value is shown as a slice of the pie.

piece fraction A *piece fraction* is constructed of small numbers and a forward slash (1/2, 1/4). 👁 Look up *built fraction* and *case fraction.*

pilcrow A *pilcrow* is the character ¶. It is used to indicate the start of a new paragraph.

PIN *PIN* is the abbreviation for **P**ersonal **I**dentification **N**umber. A PIN is a number used as a password by a computer user. 👁 Look up *password*.

piracy *Piracy* is the unauthorized copying or use of a product or service. 👁 Look up *software piracy*.

pipe (|) The *pipe* (|) is a symbol on your keyboard. It is on the backslash key (shift-backslash). Pipe commands work in MS-DOS and UNIX systems. A pipe is typically used to connect two commands so that the output from the first command becomes the input for the second command. For example, to display files in sorted order, enter DIR|SORT. 👁 Look up *backslash, command, MS-DOS,* and *UNIX*.

pixel (short for "picture element") The images on your computer screen are made up of small dots. These dots are *pixels*. 👁 Look up *computer screen* and *image*.

pixelate If you can see the pixels of an image, the image is *pixelated*. Pixelated images look like they are made of blocks and staircases. 👁 Look up *image* and *pixel*.

platform **(1)** A *platform* is a particular computer system and all of the hardware and software that work with the system.
 (2) A *platform* is a particular operating system or program. 👁 Look up *hardware, operating system, program,* and *software*.

PNG *PNG* (pronounced "ping") is a new format for compressing images. 👁 Look up *data compression, format, GIF, image,* and *JPEG*.

point **(1)** A *point* is a unit of measurement equal to about 1/72 of an inch. The abbreviation for point is pt. (always with a period). Points are used for measuring font sizes and for many other things in printing. Most book fonts are about 10 points, which is 10/72 = 5/36 of an inch tall. 👁 Look up *font size* and *pica*.
 (2) To *point* means to put the arrow or some other type of pointer on something onto your computer screen. 👁 Look up *computer screen*.

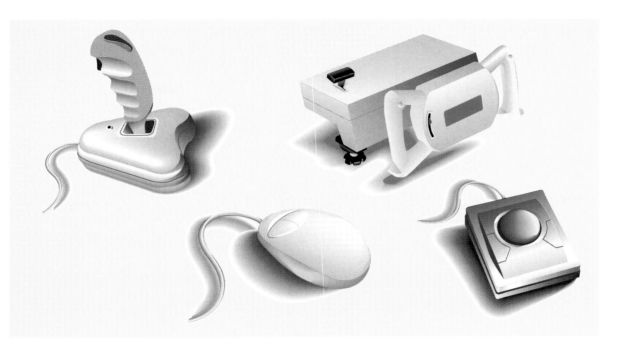

pointer A *pointer* is the arrow that you move around the screen to select things when you use a computer with a graphical user interface. ◉ Look up *graphical user interface* and *screen*.

pointing device A *pointing device* is a mouse, a trackball, a touch pad, or anything that you use to control a pointer on your computer screen. ◉ Look up *computer screen, mouse,* and *trackball*.

port (1) A *port* is what your computer uses to communicate with devices. For example, your computer uses a port to communicate with your printer.
  (2) To *port* is to transfer data from one computer to another. For example, some programs are ported from Macintosh to PC

computers. ◉ Look up *communicate, computer, data, device, Macintosh, parallel port, PC, printer,* and *serial port*.

portable computer A *portable computer* is a computer that is larger than a laptop

but small enough to be easily carried. 👁 Look up *computer* and *laptop computer.*

portal A *portal* is a web site that provides links to other sites. For example, *www.lycos. com* and *www.yahoo.com* are portals. The home pages of some Internet service providers are portals. 👁 Look up *home page, Internet service provider, link,* and *web site.*

portrait orientation A page or image has *portrait orientation* if it is longer from top to bottom than it is from left to right. 👁 Look up *image, landscape orientation,* and *orientation.*

post (1) A *post* is information shared in an on-line group or newsgroup.

(2) To *post* is to share information in an on-line group or newsgroup. 👁 Look up *information.*

PostScript *PostScript* is a computer language that creates high-resolution prints on laser printers. PostScript is an object-oriented language. This means that images are represented using geometric lines instead of bits. 👁 Look up *bit, image, laser printer, object-oriented language,* and *resolution.*

pound sign A *pound sign* is the character #.

power-down To *power-down* is to turn off a computer or some other machine.

PowerPC A *PowerPC* is a computer from a family of fast, powerful computers that can run DOS or Macintosh software. 👁 Look up *DOS, Macintosh,* and *software.*

PowerPC CPU The *PowerPC CPU* is the CPU of one series of Macintosh computers. 👁 Look up *CPU* and *Macintosh.*

power strip A *power strip* is a long, narrow box with electric outlets, a circuit breaker, and perhaps other devices to protect your computer or other electronics. Often, power strips include a surge protector.  Look up *computer, device,* and *surge protector.*

power-up To *power-up* is to turn on a computer or some other machine.

power user A *power user* is a computer user who has a lot of experience and who uses the computer for more demanding purposes than the average user. Look up *computer* and *user.*

PPL *PPL* is an abbreviation for "people." It is used in informal e-mail, chat, and Usenet.

*John: The **ppl** next door have a trampoline and pool and invited us over this weekend. Want to go?*

Juan: Sure, I'd love to go. I'll see you tomorrow.

See the appendix, pages 189–190, for a complete table of abbreviations. Look up *chat, e-mail,* and *Usenet.*

ppm Look up *pages per minute.*

prefix A *prefix* is a group of letters or symbols at the beginning of a word that changes the meaning of the word. For example, the prefix *mega-* added to the beginning of the word *byte* makes the word *megabyte.* Look up *megabyte.*

preformatted A *preformatted* disk is a disk that is formatted and ready for you to use to store data. Preformatted disks are available for PC and for Macintosh computers. Look up *data, disk,* and *format.*

printer A *printer* is a machine that prints computer output onto paper. You can use a printer to print your letters, pictures, history reports, and many other things.

printer driver A *printer driver* is a program in your computer that runs your printer. Look up *computer* and *program.*

printer stand A *printer stand* is a table designed to support a printer. Printer stands often have shelves for paper and files. 👁 Look up *printer*.

printer resolution *Printer resolution* is the quality of a printer. There used to be three different levels of quality for printers: letter quality, near-letter quality, and draft quality. Letter quality has the best resolution, and draft quality has the poorest resolution. Printer resolution is now measured in DPI. 👁 Look up *dpi* and *draft quality*.

print job A *print job* is a file that you are printing on a printer. 👁 Look up *file* and *printer*.

Print Manager The *Print Manager* is the print spooler built into Windows 3.1. A print spooler is a utility program that manages files that are sent to the printer to be printed. 👁 Look up *file, printer,* and *utility program*.

printout Information on paper that is created by a computer's instructions to a printer is a *printout*. A printout is also called a hard copy. 👁 Look up *computer* and *information*.

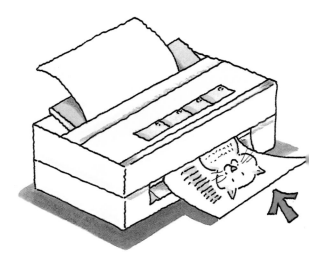

program (1) A *program* is a list of instructions that the computer follows when you play a computer game, use a word processor, send e-mail, or do anything else on your computer.

(2) To *program* is to write a program using a programming language like BASIC, C++, and many others. 👁 Look up *BASIC, e-mail, programming language, software,* and *word processing*.

programmer A *programmer* is a person who writes programs for a computer. A program is a list of instructions that the computer follows when you play a computer game, use a word processor, send e-mail, or do anything else on your computer.

👁 Look up *e-mail, program,* and *word processor.*

programming language Any language that you can use to write a list of instructions that a computer can understand is a *programming language.* For example, BASIC, C, C++, Pascal, and Java are programming languages. 👁 Look up *BASIC, C++, Java,* and *Pascal.*

prompt When a program needs information from you, it will give you some kind of signal. The signal is called a *prompt.* A prompt is very often a blinking cursor, but it can be other symbols and may have instructions. 👁 Look up *cursor, information, program,* and *symbol.*

PROMPT command If you want to change the way your prompt looks, you use the DOS *PROMPT command.* 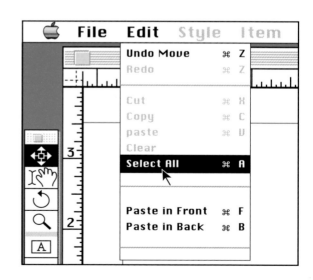 Look up *DOS* and *prompt.*

Propeller key ⌘ The *Propeller key* lets you change the meaning of other keys. This is done by pressing the Propeller key at the same time you press the key you want to change. The Propeller key is also called the command key. It is a modifier key.

---

proportionally spaced font A *proportionally spaced font* is a font in which thin letters, like *i*, take only a little space, while wide letters, like *m*, take more space. For example, Times New Roman is a proportionally spaced font, and Courier is a monospaced font. Here is the same greeting in Times New Roman and then in Courier:

Courier:
```
Hello, Milo!
```

Times New Roman:
Hello, Milo!

Notice that with Times New Roman, the letter *l*, for example, takes up less space than the letter *e*. With Courier, the space taken up by the letters is the same for each letter. 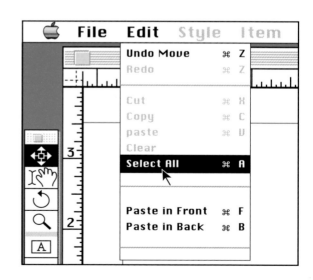 Look up *mono-spaced font.*

---

protocol A *protocol* is a way of communicating information according to an agreed-upon format. If two people want to communicate with each other, they must speak the same language. In the same way, computers must use the same protocol if they are to communicate. For example, TCP/IP is the protocol used in the Internet. 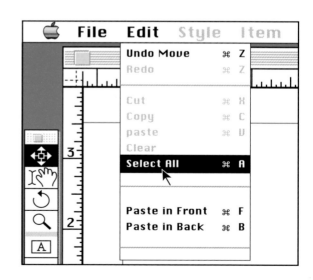 Look up *communicate, format, information, Internet,* and *TCP/IP.*

---

pt. *pt.* is an abbreviation for point. A point is about 1/72 of an inch. Points are used for measuring font sizes and for many other things in printing. Most book fonts are about 10 points, which is $10/72 = 5/36$ of an inch tall. 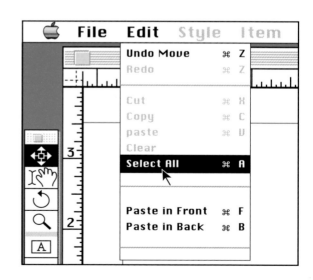 Look up *font size.*

---

pull-down menu A *pull-down menu* is a list of choices that run down the screen when you click on the menu at the top of the page. 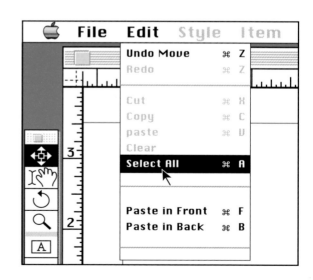 Look up *click.*

question mark (?) The *question mark* symbol ? is a wild card that stands for a single character. For example, if you type dir a?c, the computer will return files named abc, amc, azc, or any other file whose name has three letters and begins with an *a* and ends with a *c*. 👁 Look up *character* and *wild card.*

QuickDraw *QuickDraw* is a Macintosh package used to draw graphics on the monitor. The QuickDraw system can also be used in printers. 👁 Look up *image, Macintosh, monitor,* and *printer.*

QuickTime *QuickTime* is a system (and a file format) for viewing audio/video files. Many web sites have QuickTime movies that you can download and watch. 👁 Look up *download, file, format,* and *web site.*

QWERTY The *QWERTY* keyboard layout is the standard layout found on most keyboards. Its name comes from the first six letters in the upper left row of the keyboard. 👁 Look up *Dvorak* and *keyboard.*

radio button A *radio button* is a small button on a form, on a web page, or in a list of options in some programs. Radio buttons let you select an option (to select the option listed beside the button, click on the button). 👁 Look up *form* and *web site*.

Radio Shack *Radio Shack*, a division of Tandy Corporation, is a large chain of retail stores selling electronic equipment and computers. It can be located on the web at *http://www.tandy.com*.

ragged left Text in which the words that begin a line do not line up is *ragged left* text.

> This is an example of
> text with ragged
> left margin.

👁 Look up *justification* and *text*.

ragged right Text in which the words that end a line do not line up is *ragged right* text.

> This is an example of
> text with ragged
> right margin.

👁 Look up *justification* and *text*.

RAM (pronounced as a single word, "RAM") *RAM* is an acronym for **r**andom-**a**ccess **m**emory. RAM is memory in which your computer can store data and from which it can read data. RAM is the memory that your computer uses to store and retrieve data when it runs a program. RAM is different from ROM. Your computer cannot write to ROM, it can only read from ROM. 👁 Look up *data, memory, program* and *ROM*.

random-access memory (RAM) 👁 Look up *RAM*.

random number A *random number* is a number that is picked by chance with no predictable pattern. For example, the numbers

5, 13, 21, 89, 2

could be a list of random numbers. On the other hand, the numbers

1, 2, 3, 4, 5

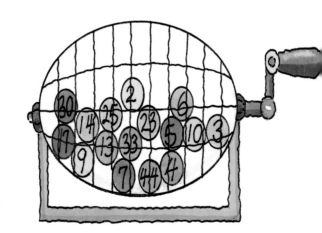

are probably not a list of random numbers. Many programming languages provide random number generators to allow for simulations of random events.

random number generator A *random number generator* lists numbers randomly. 👁 Look up *random number.*

range A *range* is a group of numbers that includes a smallest and a largest number and all numbers between. For example, 1–5 is a range of numbers. It contains the numbers 1, 2, 3, 4, 5.

ray tracing To make a computer image look more realistic, the computer can make the image reflect or absorb light. This is called *ray tracing.* To work, the user must tell the computer the exact location of the light source being simulated. 👁 Look up *computer* and *image.*

RD command 👁 Look up *remove directory command.*

RE *RE* is an abbreviation for "regards." It is used in informal e-mail, chat, and Usenet. See the appendix, pages 189–190, for a complete table of abbreviations. 👁 Look up *chat, e-mail,* and *Usenet.*

read To *read* is to get data from a storage device so that you can use it. 👁 Look up *data* and *storage device.*

readme *Readme* files are files about software that users should read before using the software. Readme files often include notes about changes or corrections to the current version of the software program. 👁 Look up *file, software, user,* and *version number.*

read-only Information in a computer that can be seen on your monitor but cannot be changed without first entering a special code is *read-only* information. 👁 Look up *information* and *monitor.*

read-only memory (ROM) 👁 Look up *ROM.*

read/write head A *read/write head* is a device inside a disk drive that reads data from the surface of a disk when you load a file and writes data to the surface of the disk when you save a file. 👁 Look up *data, device, disk drive,* and *seek time.*

ream A *ream* is a package of paper that has 500 sheets.

reboot To *reboot* a computer means to restart the computer. This can be done using a special command, or some computers have a reset button for this purpose. 👁 Look up *command*.

recover (1) To *recover* is to restore information that has been erased or lost. 👁 Look up *information*.

(2) To *recover* is to return a computer from not working correctly to working as it should.

Recycle Bin The *Recycle Bin* stores deleted files in versions of Windows beginning with Windows 95. 👁 Look up *file* and *Microsoft Windows*.

Refresh button The *Refresh button* is a button on web browsers that updates your view of a web page.

When should I use the Refresh button? Anytime that you want the server to resend the web page that you are viewing to make sure that you are getting the most recent version of the page and not a cached copy. 👁 Look up *browser, cache, server,* and *web page*.

regional settings *Regional settings* are settings in a system that relate to the geographical location of the user. Examples include language, currency, and time zone.

registration card A *registration card* is a form that comes with computer products. It should be filled out and returned to the manufacturer so you will be eligible for help using the product and for other things, such as information about upgrades. 👁 Look up *upgrade*.

remove directory command The *remove directory command* tells your computer that you want to delete a directory. The DOS command is RD (name of directory), Enter or RMDIR (name of directory), Enter. The directory to be deleted must be empty. ◉ Look up *command* and *directory.*

....

required hyphen A *required hyphen* is a hyphen that does not mark a place where a word can be broken onto separate lines. A word with a required hyphen cannot be split at the hyphen.

....

reset button The *reset button* is a button that restarts your computer. Memory is cleared when you press the reset button. ◉ Look up *computer* and *memory.*

....

resident font A *resident font* is a font that is built into the hardware of a printer. ◉ Look up *hardware* and *printer.*

....

resolution **(1)** The *resolution* is the amount of detail that you can see on a screen or on a printed page. The greater

the resolution, the greater the detail that you can see.

(2) As applied to monitors, *resolution* is a measure of the numbers of pixels that can be displayed (width × height).

(3) As applied to printers, *resolution* is often a measure of dots per inch.

....

restart To *restart* a computer means to reboot the computer after it has been turned on. ◉ Look up *reboot.*

....

restore To *restore* is to return a window to its original size on your computer screen after it has been minimized or maximized. In versions of Windows beginning with Windows 95, the restore button is on the title bar in the upper right corner of the screen. ◉ Look up *maximize, minimize, Microsoft Windows,* and *title bar.*

....

retrieve To *retrieve* something is to get it so that it can be used. When a computer retrieves a file or a folder, it transfers the file or folder from a storage device, such as a disk drive, to its memory so that the file can be used. ◉ Look up *disk drive, file, folder, memory,* and *storage device.*

....

Return key **(1)** The *Return key*, or Enter key, tells your computer that you want it to accept and process as input something that you have typed.

(2) The *Return key* makes the cursor return to the beginning of the next line. ◉ Look up *cursor.*

....

RGB color *RGB color* is color made by combining red, green, and blue.

right arrow key The *right arrow key* moves the cursor one space to the right.

right-click To *right-click* means to press the button on the right side of the mouse, trackball, touch pad, or other input device. 👁 Look up *input device, mouse,* and *track-ball.*

right justified Text in which the last words of each line are lined up is *right justified.* 👁 Look up *text.*

Rio The *Rio* is a portable MP3 audio file player. MP3 files are a kind of audio file. The Rio is made by Diamond Multimedia. 👁 Look up *audio file, file,* and *MP3.*

RISC *RISC* is an abbreviation for **R**educed **I**nstruction **S**et **C**omputer. The RISC system simplifies and lowers the number of instructions the microprocessor can exe-

cute. This increases processing speed and makes a faster computer. 👁 Look up *microprocessor.*

.rm The suffix *.rm* means that a file is a RealVideo movie. 👁 Look up *file.*

rm *rm* is a UNIX command that instructs the computer to delete a file. 👁 Look up *file* and *UNIX.*

RMDIR command 👁 Look up *remove directory command.*

robot A *robot* is a machine that does some things that humans can do. 👁 Look up *machine.*

ROFL *ROFL* is an abbreviation for "rolling on the floor laughing." It is used in informal e-mail, chat, and Usenet. See the appendix, pages 189–190, for a complete table of abbreviations. 👁 Look up *chat, e-mail,* and *Usenet.*

rollover A *rollover* is a message that appears when the mouse curser passes over a key word, icon, or graphic even though the mouse has not been clicked. 👁 Look up *mouse* and *mouse cursor.*

ROM (pronounced as a single word, "ROM") *ROM* is an acronym for **r**ead-**o**nly **m**emory. Memory that can be read from but cannot be changed is ROM. ROM is usu-

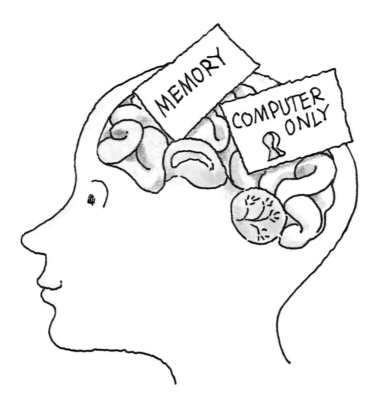

ally stored in a computer chip. Look up *information, memory,* and *RAM.*

Roman *Roman* is the style of type that books are usually set in, as distinguished from bold or italics. Look up *bold, italics,* and *typeface.*

rotate To *rotate* is to turn, as the wheels on a bicycle turn. When you use art programs, you can rotate an image.

ROTFL *ROTFL* is an abbreviation for "rolling on the floor laughing." It is used in informal e-mail, chat, and Usenet. See the appendix, pages 189–190, for a complete table of abbreviations. Look up *chat, e-mail,* and *Usenet.*

root directory The *root directory* is the first, or top-level, directory in a file system. Look up *directory.*

row A *row* is a horizontal line of data. Look up *data.*

RSN *RSN* is the abbreviation for "real soon now." It is used in informal e-mail, chat, and Usenet.

Peg: I have been waiting for you to send me the directions to that restaurant for weeks. Am I ever going to get them?
Max: **rsn**. *I will send them as soon as I remember where I wrote them down.*

See the appendix on pages 189–190, for a complete table of abbreviations. ◉ Look up *chat, e-mail, and Usenet.*

RTFM *RTFM* is an abbreviation for "read the friendly manual." It is used in informal e-mail, chat, and Usenet.

John: I've tried for three hours to hook up my new train system, and I just can't.
Juan: I know that you don't want to, but if you would **rtfm**, *it will tell you step-by-step how to do it.*

See the appendix, pages 189–190, for a complete table of abbreviations. ◉ Look up *chat, e-mail,* and *Usenet.*

RUMOF *RUMOF* is an abbreviation for "are you male or female?" It is used in informal e-mail, chat, and Usenet. See the appendix, pages 189–190, for a complete table of abbreviations. ◉ Look up *chat, e-mail,* and *Usenet.*

---

run To *run* a program means to tell a computer to start a program. When a program runs, the computer reads the program and follows the program's instructions to do something. ◉ Look up *computer* and *program.*

RYFM *RYFM* is an abbreviation for "read your friendly manual." It is used in informal e-mail, chat, and Usenet.

John: I just can't get this new program up and running.
Juan: **ryfm**.

See the appendix, pages 189–190, for a complete table of abbreviations. ◉ Look up *chat, e-mail,* and *Usenet.*

Sad Mac A *Sad Mac* is the sad face that you see on a Macintosh computer when something is wrong. 👁 Look up *Happy Mac* and *Macintosh.*

sandbox A child's *sandbox* is a place to build castles, drive toy cars, and have a good time. Sandboxes have walls that separate them from the rest of a playground. When you use computers and the Internet, you may want to run a program, but you may be afraid that the program will do something that will damage your computer. A sandbox is a feature that lets you run a program but allows the program to do only safe things. This way you can run the program without having to worry that it will do something to harm your computer. 👁 Look up *Internet* and *program.*

sans serif Letters in books, newspapers, and magazines usually have lines at the ends of the curves that form them. These lines are called serifs. Sometimes the letters do not have these lines. Letters that do not have serifs are called *sans serif*. Shown are some words made using sans serif letters. Look at the letters in the words, and you can see that no small lines appear on the ends of the letters. 👁 Look up *serif.*

Avant Garde
Franklin Gothic
Futura
Univers

save To *save* means to copy information onto a disk. For example, when you are typing a letter or report on a word processor, you should save the file often so that you will not lose any of your work should something unexpected happen.  Look up *backup, copy, disk, file,* and *word processor.*

scan To *scan* is to transfer information from a page into a computer's memory. This is done by exposing the page to a device that turns the information into digital form and enters it into the computer. Look up *device, hand scanner, memory,* and *scanner.*

scanner You can use your computer to work with images, but you must first input the image into your computer. A *scanner* is a device that lets you input images. Some

printers are also scanners, and other scanners are operated by hand. Look up *computer, device, hand scanner,* and *image.*

screen The *screen* is the part of your computer on which information is displayed. The size of the screen is measured from corner to corner. Look up *information* and *monitor.*

screen dump If you have something on your computer screen that you want to save, you can do a *screen dump,* and the computer will make a printout of the computer screen. Many programs have an icon that you can click to do a screen dump. Look up *save* and *screen.*

screen resolution *Screen resolution* is how many pixels are on a screen. The higher the screen resolution, the higher the quality of images on the screen. Look up *image, pixel, resolution,* and *screen.*

screen saver A *screen saver* is a program that shows some simple animation on your computer screen when you are not using your computer. If you leave your computer on for too long with the same image on the screen, ghosting may happen. A faint outline, or ghost, of the image that you leave displayed will be left on your screen. You can use a screen saver to keep ghosting from happening. Some screen savers look like aquariums, some are stars twinkling, and some are strange geometric objects moving and changing. Many other screen savers are available. 👁 Look up *burn-in, ghosting, program,* and *screen.*

script *Script* is a style of type that looks like cursive handwriting.

This sentence is in a script type.

scroll **(1)** Words or images that move on your computer screen, either horizontally or vertically, are said to *scroll.*

(2) When you *scroll* a document or an image, you move it so that you can see other parts of it. You usually do this by using a slide bar or a scrolling wheel. 👁 Look up *image, screen, scroll bar,* and *scrolling wheel.*

scroll bar The *scroll bar* is a bar on the side and bottom of a window that is used for scrolling a document or image. Scroll bars are used to move a documents or images around to see all of them. 👁 Look up *image, scroll,* and *window.*

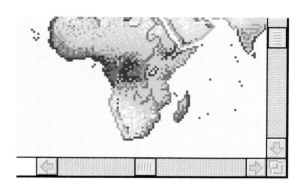

scrolling wheel A *scrolling wheel* is a wheel on mice and other pointing devices that lets you scroll through information on a computer screen. Scrolling wheels are especially useful when you view web pages. 👁 Look up *mouse, pointing device,* and *web page.*

SCSI (pronounced "scuzzy") *SCSI* is an abbreviation for **s**mall **c**omputer **s**ystems **i**nterface. SCSI allows your computer to communicate with devices. 👁 Look up *computer* and *device.*

seamless *Seamless* means smooth operation without any problems. For example, if two programs work together with no problems whatsoever, then you can say that they work together seamlessly. When information is transferred from one computer system to another with no errors, then you can say that the transfer was seamless. 👁 Look up *computer* and *program.*

search engine A *search engine* is a program that lets you search the World Wide Web for information that you want to view. Search sites like those in the table below have search engines that you can use.

Search Site	URL
Lycos	http://www.lycos.com
Infoseek	http://www.infoseek.com
WebCrawler	http://www.webcrawler.com
Yahoo!	http://www.yahoo.com
Excite	http://www.excite.com
AltaVista	http://www.altavista.com

👁 Look up *information, URL,* and *World Wide Web.*

Searchware *Searchware* is a type of software that searches through a database. Reference works available on CD-ROM, such as encyclopedias, must contain searchware so that users can find specific items. 👁 Look up *database* and *software.*

section sign A *section sign* is the symbol §. It indicates different parts of text or of a document. It is frequently used in legal documents.

seek time *Seek time* is the amount of time the read/write head of a disk drive takes to move from one track of a disk to another track. 👁 Look up *disk drive* and *read/write head.*

semiconductor A *semiconductor* is a special material, usually silicon, that can be used to make transistors, which are the building blocks of CPUs, memory chips, and other internal parts of a computer. 👁 Look up *computer, CPU, memory,* and *silicon.*

sentence fragment A *sentence fragment* is a group of words that is missing a subject, a verb, or both. For example, "all the men on the boat" is a sentence fragment, because it does not have a verb. Although the words draw our attention to all of the men on a boat, they do not tell us anything about the men. On the other hand, the words "all the men on the boat were seasick" is a sentence.

serial port A *serial port* is a type of port. With a serial port, data is transmitted one bit at a time. 👁 Look up *bit, data, parallel port, port,* and *printer.*

serif Letters in books, newspapers, and magazines usually have lines at the ends of the curves that form them. These lines are called *serifs.* Shown are some words made using serif letters. Look at the letters, and you can see small lines on the ends of the letters. 👁 Look up *sans serif*.

Century Old Style
Courier
Garamond
Times Bold

server A *server* is a computer or a program that provides data to a client, which is a program that receives the data. For example, a web browser receives data from a server. 👁 Look up *browser, client, data,* and *program.*

service provider A *service provider* is a company that provides computer or networking services to its clients. 👁 Look up *access provider* and *Internet.*

session A *session* is the length of time that a service is used.

setup program A *setup program* is a program that enters information about a configuration into a computer. 👁 Look up *computer* and *information.*

shareware *Shareware* is copyrighted software that you can use for a while for free. If you like the software and continue to use it, then you are supposed to pay a fee to the programmer or the company that owns it. Shareware is a little like sharing a free soda with a friend. If you want more than is being given away, you are expected to pay. 👁 Look up *programmer* and *software.*

Shockwave *Shockwave* is a system for multimedia on the World Wide Web. Shockwave is owned by Macromedia, Inc. ◉ Look up *mulitmedia, system,* and *World Wide Web.*

shortcut On Windows computers, a *shortcut* is an icon that lets you easily open a file, a folder, or a program. The shortcut icon is a special icon that connects you to items represented by other icons. For example, a program may have an icon in a folder on your hard drive. You can make a shortcut icon and put it onto your desktop so that you can run the program by clicking the icon on your desktop. Macintosh computers have a similar feature called an alias. ◉ Look up *alias, click, desktop, file, folder, hard drive, icon, Macintosh, program,* and *Windows.*

showstopper A *showstopper* is a bug in a program that is so serious that the maker has to delay production. ◉ Look up *bug* and *program.*

shut down To *shut down* a computer means to turn the computer off.

SIG *SIG* is an acronym for **s**pecial **i**nterest **g**roup. SIGs use computer services to meet and discuss specific things. ◉ Look up *special interest group.*

silicon *Silicon* is a special material used to make transistors, which are the building blocks of CPUs, memory chips, and other internal parts of a computer. ◉ Look up *CPU* and *memory.*

silicon chip A *silicon chip* is a small rectangular chip made of silicon on which circuits are etched. These circuits are the brains and memory of your computer. ◉ Look up *circuit, computer, memory,* and *silicon.*

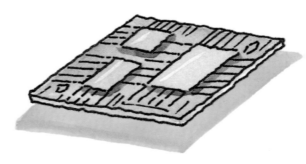

simulation   A *simulation* is a computer model of something in the real world.

What kinds of things do people simulate using computers? All kinds of things are simulated on computers. For example, meteorologists simulate the weather, engineers simulate engines so that they can design them better, and economists simulate the economy. 👁 Look up *random number.*

---

single click   To *single click* is to press a mouse button only once. 👁 Look up *mouse.*

---

site   *Site* is short for web site. 👁 Look up *web site.*

---

slash   A *slash* is the character / on a keyboard. 👁 Look up *keyboard.*

---

slider   (1) A *slider* is the button in a scroll bar that moves up and down or side to side to show other parts of a picture. Sliders are also used for other things, such as adjusting volume. 👁 Look up *scroll bar.*

(2) A *slider* is the tab used to write-protect a diskette. 👁 Look up *diskette* and *write protect.*

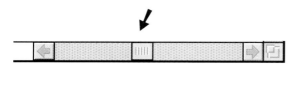

---

slot   A *slot* is short for expansion slot. An expansion slot is an opening in a computer that is designed to take a printed circuit board. The printed circuit board allows the computer to perform additional functions. 👁 Look up *circuit board* and *computer.*

---

small caps   *Small caps* is a type style that uses normal-sized uppercase letters for capitals and small uppercase letters for lowercase letters. Small caps style is also called cap and small style. 👁 Look up *lowercase* and *uppercase.*

> THE CAPITAL OF PENNSYLVANIA IS HARRISBURG.

<SMALL> tag   The *<SMALL> tag* is an HTML tag that makes text smaller than the other text on a web page. 👁 Look up *HTML, tag,* and *web page.*

---

smiley   The symbols :) and :-) are *smiley* faces. You can use these symbols in your e-mail or whenever you are communicating by computer to show that you are happy. A smiley is an emoticon. There are also sad face emotions, bored face emoticons, and many others. 👁 Look up *communicate, e-mail,* and *emoticon.*

---

snail mail   Sometimes people use the term *snail mail* for the ordinary mail that the post office delivers for you. Snails are slow, and people sometimes call ordinary mail snail mail to imply that it is slower than e-mail. ◉ Look up *e-mail*.

sneaker net   When people walk from computer to computer carrying diskettes to transfer files instead of transferring them over an electronic network, they are a *sneaker net*. ◉ Look up *computer, diskette, file,* and *network*.

soft copy   A *soft copy* of data is data on a monitor that you look at or data stored in memory. ◉ Look up *data, memory,* and *monitor.*

soft font   A *soft font* is a font that exists in a printer's memory and is used by a program. ◉ Look up *memory, printer,* and *program.*

soft hyphen   A *soft hyphen* is used only to break up a word when it falls at the end of a line. ◉ Look up *required hyphen.*

software   *Software* is a program or programs that you can run on your computer. Video games, word processors, and browsers, for example, are software. ◉ Look up *browser, computer, program,* and *word processor.*

software company   A *software company* is a company that makes software for you to use on your computer. ◉ Look up *computer* and *software.*

software house   ◉ Look up *software company.*

software license   A *software license* is an agreement between a computer user and a software maker about what the user may and may not do with the software. Usually, the user agrees, among other things, not to copy or to share the software with others who have not paid for it. ◉ Look up *computer, software,* and *user.*

software package A *software package* is a program that is complete and prepared to run. Any necessary documentation and utility programs are included in a software package. ◉ Look up *documentation, program,* and *utility program.*

software piracy Pirates captured ships on the high seas and stole their cargo. *Software piracy* is when software pirates steal programs by making illegal copies. ◉ Look up *program* and *software.*

software program *Software program* means program. A program is a list of instructions that the computer follows when you play a computer game, use a word processor, send e-mail, or do anything else on a computer. ◉ Look up *e-mail* and *word processor.*

software publisher A *software publisher* owns, publishes, and sells computer software. ◉ Look up *computer* and *software.*

sort To *sort* is to arrange a list in some order. Usually, the list is arranged in numerical or alphabetical order.

Sound Blaster *Sound Blaster* is a popular line of sound cards for personal computers. ◉ Look up *personal computer* and *sound card.*

sound card A *sound card* is a circuit board that you can add to your computer so that it can create and play sound effects. ◉ Look up *circuit board* and *computer.*

source disk A *source disk* is a storage disk that holds information that can be copied to another storage device. ◉ Look up *device, disk,* and *storage device.*

spaghetti code A program that is poorly written and not well structured is *spaghetti code.* ◉ Look up *program.*

special interest group A *special interest group* is a group of people interested in the same topic who meet in person or through a computer oline service. 👁 Look up *online.*

speech recognition *Speech recognition* is the ability of a computer system to identify spoken words.

speech synthesis *Speech synthesis* is the using of a computer to make words. Speech synthesis lets your computer talk, but it can say only what it is programmed to say. Speech synthesis uses computer-created sound, not recordings. 👁 Look up *computer* and *program.*

spell checker A *spell checker* is a program that checks for mistakes in your spelling by comparing a word that you type to words in a dictionary that are part of the spell checker program. Spell checkers do not identify mistakes when words are spelled correctly but used incorrectly. For example, a spell checker will not choose between *their*, *there*, and *they're*, although a grammar checker might. 👁 Look up *program*.

spreadsheet A *spreadsheet* is a program that lets you input rows and columns of numbers into a table so that you can store data and do calculations. People use spreadsheets for many things, including accounting and taxes. 👁 Look up *program*.

	A	B	C	D
1	cell A1	cell B1		
2				cell D2
3			cell C3	

sprite A *sprite* is a programmable object. The characters, spaceships, fireballs, and other moving objects in video games, for example, are usually programmed using sprites. 👁 Look up *program*.

star 👁 Look up *asterisk*.

StartUp folder A *StartUp folder* is part of the Microsoft Windows system. A program placed into the Startup window will start every time you start your computer. 👁 Look up *folder* and *Microsoft Windows.*

Startup Items folder A *Startup Items folder* is a folder on Macintosh computers that contains a set of programs that always run when the computer is started. 👁 Look up *Macintosh* and *program.*

Stop button The *Stop button* is a button on most web browsers. The Stop button stops your browser from accessing a page that you have begun to access. 👁 Look up *Back button, browser, Forward button,* and *Home button.*

storage *Storage* is the amount of information that computer memory can hold or that a disk can hold. 👁 Look up *disk, information,* and *memory.*

storage device A *storage device* is any device that your computer can use to store programs or data. For example, hard disk drives, floppy disks, and CD-ROM players are storage devices. 👁 Look up *CD-ROM player, data, device, floppy disk,* and *program.*

streaming A *streaming* audio or video file is a file that you can begin listening to or

viewing while you are downloading it. This saves you the time used waiting for the file to download completely before viewing it. 👁 Look up *download* and *file.*

subdirectory A *subdirectory* is a directory that is held inside another directory. 👁 Look up *directory.*

suffix (1) A *suffix* is a group of letters or symbols at the end of a word that changes the meaning of the word.

(2) In computer file names, a *suffix* is a group of letters or symbols at the end of a word that denotes the type of file. For example, the suffix .jpg in the file name

myselfportrait.jpg

means that the file is a JPEG image, which you can view. 👁 Look up *file, image,* and *JPEG.*

suitcase A *suitcase* is a set of system resources held in a special folder on the Macintosh. 👁 Look up *folder*.

Sun Microsystems, Inc. This company, which developed Sun workstations, microprocessors, operating systems, and the Java programming language, can be found on the web at *http://www.sun.com*

supercomputer A *supercomputer* is a computer that uses parallel processing to operate much faster than other computers. 👁 Look up *parallel processing*.

SuperDrive A *SuperDrive* is a high-density disk drive that comes with Macintosh computers. The SuperDrive reads and writes to all Macintosh disks. 👁 Look up *density, disk drive,* and *Macintosh*.

superscript Characters or symbols that are raised and smaller than normal characters are *superscript*. 👁 Look up *symbol*.

Super VGA monitor A *Super VGA monitor* is a monitor that shows information in color with high resolution. 👁 Look up *information, monitor,* and *VGA monitor*.

surf the net To *surf the net* means to explore the World Wide Web by clicking on link after link that you find interesting. ◉ Look up *click, link,* and *World Wide Web.*

surge A *surge* in an increase in power from an AC outlet. A surge can damage your computer. A surge protector can protect your computer. ◉ Look up *surge protector.*

surge protector A *surge protector* protects your computer from an electric surge. Some surge protectors are attached to extension cords. Some have on-off switches and circuit breakers.

SVGA ◉ Look up *Super VGA monitor.*

symbol A *symbol* is a shape that has a meaning. The letters of the alphabet and the other shapes on the keys of your keyboard are symbols. Very often, though, when people say symbol, they mean only the nonalphabetic and nonnumeric shapes:

~ ! @ # $ % ^ & * ( ) [{] } / ? = + \ |

These shapes are on the keys near the top of your keyboard. ◉ Look up *keyboard.*

sysop The word *sysop* is an acronym for **sys**tem **op**erator. The sysop is the person who operates a BBS (bulletin board system). ◉ Look up *acronym* and *BBS.*

system A *system* is a group of things that work together to do something.

system 6 *System 6* is an older version of the Macintosh operating system.  Look up *Macintosh* and *operating system.*

system 7 *System 7* is a newer, but not current, version of the Macintosh operating system. The current operating system is known as Mac OS. Look up *Mac OS, Macintosh,* and *operating system.*

system clock The *system clock* is a circuit that pulses at a very fast, regular rate. Your computer uses these pulses to help put its activities into the right order. Look up *circuit.*

system folder In a Macintosh computer, the system and finder files are located in the *system folder*. Also in the system folder are all the desktop accessories. Look up *folder* and *Macintosh.*

system requirements The least powerful computer and/or software that can run a program or an accessory is called the *system requirements*. Programs often require a minimum of processor speed, RAM, ROM, disk space, and other requirements. Look up *program* and *software.*

system software All the files that your computer needs to work are called the *system software*. The system software alone may not be enough to run many application programs. Look up *application program, file,* and *software.*

systems program A *systems program* is a program that your computer uses to do essential things. For example, an operating system is a systems program. Without systems programs, your computer would not run at all. Look up *Mac OS, Microsoft Windows, operating system,* and *program.*

tag A *tag* is a code used in the source of an HTML document. Your web browser reads tags to display the text and images of a web page appropriately. 👁 Look up *browser, HTML, image, text,* and *web page.*

Tagged Image File Format 👁 Look up *TIFF.*

TAN *TAN* is an acronym for **t**iny-**a**rea **n**etwork. 👁 Look up *acronym* and *tiny-area network.*

target disk A *target disk* is a disk to which information is being copied. 👁 Look up *disk.*

taskbar In Microsoft Windows, a bar appears on your screen (usually at the bottom) and tells you what programs are running. This bar is the *taskbar.* The taskbar also contains the Start menu. 👁 Look up *program, Microsoft Windows, multitasking,* and *screen.*

TCP/IP *TCP/IP* is an abbreviation for **T**ransmission **C**ontrol **P**rotocol/**I**nternet **P**rotocol. TCP/IP is the protocol that computers on the Internet use to communicate with each other so that you can view web pages, download files, and so on. TCP/IP is a list of specific rules for organizing files and for sending and receiving files over the Internet. 👁 Look up *download, Internet,* and *web page.*

technical writer A *technical writer* is a person who writes technical materials, such as instruction manuals for computers and software products. 👁 Look up *computer* and *software.*

telecommute To work from a home office using a computer, modem, fax, telephone, and other electronic devices is to *telecommute.* 👁 Look up *fax, modem.*

template Cookies in the shape of animals are made by putting cookie dough into special pans with sections that are shaped like animals. A *template* is a pattern that helps you to make something like a letter or a graphics image, just like a pan with animal shapes helps you to make animal-shaped cookies. Many word-processing programs come with templates for things like letters, announcements, holidays, and birthday cards. To use these templates, you find the appropriate one for what you are doing and then enter your own specific information. 👁 Look up *image* and *word processor.*

tera- *tera-* is a prefix meaning one trillion (1,000,000,000,000). In computer and Internet terminology, it means 1,099,511,627,776 (which equals 2^{40}). 👁 Look up *kilo-, mega-,* and *prefix.*

terabyte A *terabyte* is about one trillion (1,000,000,000,000) bytes. (It is exactly 1,099,511,627,776 bytes.) 👁 Look up *byte, kilobyte,* and *megabyte.*

Texas Instruments The integrated circuit necessary to miniaturize electronic equipment was developed in the late 1950s by *Texas Instruments.* Today, Texas Instruments produces parts for almost all types of computers. It can be located on the web at *http://www.ti.com.* 👁 Look up *integrated circuit.*

text Words, letters, numbers, and symbols, such as !, @, #, and so on, are called *text.* 👁 Look up *symbol.*

text editor A *text editor* is a program designed to change or correct text. 👁 Look up *program* and *text.*

thumbnail A *thumbnail* is a small image of a larger image. 👁 Look up *image* and *web page.*

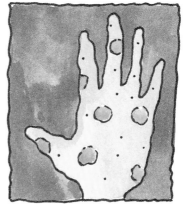

TIA *TIA* is an abbreviation for "thanks in advance." It is used in informal e-mail, chat, and Usenet.

> Jane: **tia** *for giving me a ride to my friend's house. My parents are out of town, and I don't want to miss the birthday party tonight.*
> Mary: *No problem.*

See the appendix, pages 189–190, for a complete table of abbreviations. 👁 Look up *chat, e-mail,* and *Usenet.*

tickler A *tickler* is a program that checks the computer system for dates and then informs the user about appointments and events that are upcoming. 👁 Look up *program* and *user.*

TIF *tif* is a suffix that indicates that a file is a TIFF file. 👁 Look up *suffix* and *TIFF.*

TIFF (pronounced as a single word, "tiff") *TIFF* is an acronym for **T**agged **I**mage **F**ile **F**ormat. It is a file format for compressing images. Images usually take up a lot of memory. TIFF compresses them so that they do not take up so much space. 👁 Look up *compression, file, image, JPEG,* and *web site.*

tight Type that is set so closely that the letters practically touch is said to be *tight.*

tilde A *tilde* is the character ~. In web addresses it is used to indicate the home directory of a user. For example, *~berry* is the home directory of the user named berry.

TIME command The DOS *TIME command* lets you see the time that is kept by your computer. The TIME command also allows you to set the time. To check the time, type TIME (Enter). To set the time, type TIME (time to be set) (Enter). 👁 Look up *command* and *computer.*

tint A *tint* is a shade of a color that is expressed as a percent of the actual color.

tiny-area network (TAN) A *tiny-area network* is a network of two or three computers. The computers would usually be in the same room. A TAN is smaller than a LAN because LANs are usually at least a few dozen computers in one building. Some video games can be linked together by a cable so that two players can play at the same time. This use is an example of a TAN. 👁 Look up *Internet, local-area network, network,* and *wide-area network.*

title bar A *title bar* is a bar at the top of a window that includes the name of the open file and standard commands that let you do things with the file. 👁 Look up *command, file,* and *windows.*

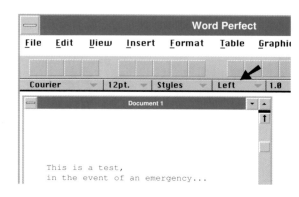

TLA *TLA* is the abbreviation for "three-letter abbreviation." It is used in informal e-mail, chat, and Usenet.

*Max: Do you know the **tla** for the new electronics store on Bay Avenue?*

Sally: Yes, I do. It's VBE—Very Best Electric.

See the appendix, pages 189–190, for a complete table of abbreviations.  Look up *chat, e-mail,* and *Usenet.*

TNX *TNX* is an abbreviation for "thanks." It is used in informal e-mail, chat, and Usenet. See the appendix, pages 189–190, for a complete table of abbreviations. Look up *chat, e-mail,* and *Usenet.*

toggle **(1)** A *toggle* is a switch that has only two settings, on and off.
   (2) To *toggle* means to change a two-setting switch from one setting to another.

toner *Toner* is the black powder that laser printers and copiers use to make images and text on a sheet of paper. Toner is made of tiny black plastic particles that are heated and fused to the paper to form images and text. Look up *image, printer,* and *text.*

toner cartridge A *toner cartridge* is a replaceable container that holds toner. Laser printers and copiers must have a toner cartridge in order to print. Look up *printer* and *toner.*

tool A *tool* gives the mouse cursor new functions and abilities. In a paint program, the cursor can act as a paintbrush and in a draw program it can act as a pencil and an eraser. Look up *draw program, mouse cursor,* and *paint program.*

touch screen A *touch screen* is a special screen that is sensitive to human touch. You can use a touch screen to enter data into a computer. Look up *computer* and *data.*

tower A *tower* is a computer enclosure that is tall and narrow. It can be placed beside the monitor on the desktop or on the floor. Frequently, a tower has more room for add-in cards and extra drives. Look up *monitor.*

trackball A *trackball* is a device that you use instead of a mouse to move the mouse pointer around the computer screen. A trackball has a ball that you move to move the mouse pointer. When you use a mouse, on the other hand, you move the mouse itself around on a mat to control the mouse pointer. Some people prefer trackballs because they say that trackballs are more comfortable to use than mice. ● Look up *device, mouse, mouse pointer,* and *screen.*

tracking *Tracking* is the spacing between letters in words.

tractor feed A *tractor feed* is a device that pulls connected sheets of paper through a dot-matrix printer. Paper for these kinds of printers has thin strips along each side that the tractor feed uses to guide the paper through the printer. ● Look up *device, dot-matrix printer,* and *printer.*

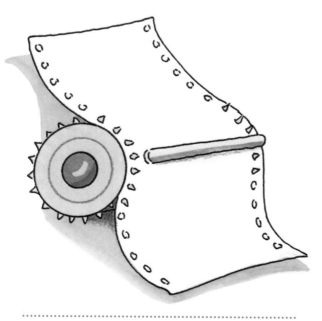

trademark A trademark is a name that only one company can use. When you use computers and the Internet, you will see many trademarks. This is because many companies have developed products and services for computers and the Internet. These companies do not want other companies to use the names of their products and services. To have the right to use a trademark, you must register it with the government of the country where the name is developed. Most governments recognize one another's trademark rules. ● Look up *computer* and *Internet.*

transfer rate The rate at which data moves from one place to another is the *transfer rate.* The transfer rate of a CD-ROM drive is crucial because the data must reach the processor fast enough to be played back without pauses. ● Look up *CPU* and *CD-ROM player.*

transistor A *transistor* is an electronic device that acts like a switch. Transistors are the most important building block of a computer. Many advances in computer technology came as engineers developed ways to build smaller and smaller transistors and put more and more of them onto chips. ● Look up *computer* and *device.*

Trash On Macintosh computers, the *Trash* file holds unwanted files. To put files into the Trash, drag the file onto the Trash icon. The file is usually not gone until the trash is emptied. On PC computers, the Recycle Bin is used for this purpose. 👁 Look up *file* and *Macintosh.*

Trekkie A *Trekkie* is a fan of the *Star Trek* television series. Many computer and Internet enthusiasts are also Trekkies. 👁 Look up *computer* and *Internet.*

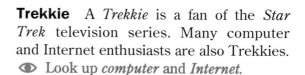

TREE command The *TREE command* is a DOS command that instructs your computer to display all the subdirectories and files beneath a directory. 👁 Look up *file, directory,* and *DOS command.*

Trojan horse A *Trojan horse* is a program that outwardly seems harmless but contains a program that can disable or destroy some part of a computer. 👁 Look up *program* and *virus.*

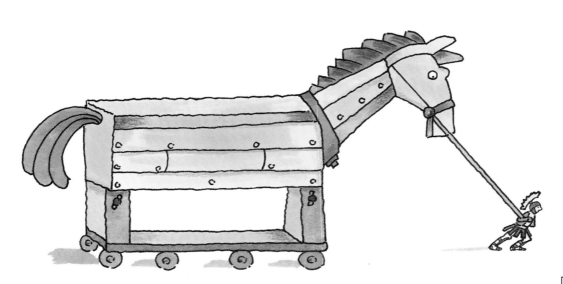

troubleshoot To *troubleshoot* is to search for the reason why something is not working properly. Sometimes a professional troubleshooter is required to fix a computer.

troubleshooter A *troubleshooter* is a person who knows how to find problems that cause devices to malfunction. 👁 Look up *malfunction.*

TrueType font A *TrueType font* is a font with letters that can be scaled to any size. TrueType was developed by Apple Computer, Incorporated. 👁 Look up *Apple Computer, Incorporated.*

TTFN *TTFN* is an abbreviation for "ta ta for now." It is used in informal e-mail, chat, and Usenet. See the appendix, pages 189–190, for a complete table of abbreviations. 👁 Look up *chat, e-mail,* and *Usenet.*

<TT> tag The *<TT> tag* is an HTML tag that makes type that looks like it was made on a typewriter. 👁 Look up *HTML* and *tag.*

TTYL *TTYL* is an abbreviation for "talk to you later." It is used in informal e-mail, chat, and Usenet.

> *John: I have to go walk my dog,* **ttyl***.*
> *Jane: Bye.*

See the appendix, pages 189–190, for a complete table of abbreviations. 👁 Look up *chat, e-mail,* and *Usenet.*

twisted pair *Twisted pair* is the name of a type of telephone line. Two lines of copper wire are wrapped around each other in the same way that two white, fuzzy cleaners are wrapped around each other to make a pipe cleaner. The twisted pair telephone line is then covered by plastic or rubber, so it looks like an electric cord or a small cable.

TYPE command The *TYPE command* is a DOS command used to display text files. 👁 Look up *file* and *text.*

typeface A *typeface* is a specific type of lettering (a font family) used on a computer printer. 👁 Look up *printer.*

UGTBK *UGTBK* is an abbreviation for "you have got to be kidding." It is used in informal e-mail, chat, and Usenet. See the appendix, pages 189–190, for a complete table of abbreviations. 👁 Look up *chat, e-mail,* and *Usenet.*

<U> tag The *<U> tag* is an HTML tag that makes underlined text. 👁 Look up *HTML, tag,* and *text.*

UI *UI* is the abbreviation for **u**ser **i**nterface. The user interface is the part of a computer program that is visible to the user and that the user interacts with. For example, the appearance of screens and menus are part of the user interface. 👁 Look up *menu, screen,* and *user interface.*

UNDELETE command In DOS, the *UNDELETE command* tells your computer to bring back a file that has been deleted. 👁 Look up *command* and *DOS.*

underlined A word or group of words is *underlined* if it has a line beneath it. On web sites, links to other sites are often under-

lined. You can click on these links to go to the site. ◉ Look up *click, hyperlink,* and *web site.*

undo The *undo* command causes a computer to reverse the effects of, or undo, the most recent operation it has performed. ◉ Look up *command.*

universal product code The *universal product code,* or UPC, is the code that you see on bags of potato chips, cans of soda,

ISBN 0-8120-9079-9

51495>

9 780812 090796

and most other items that are sold at stores. The UPC identifies the item for the store's computer.

UNIX *UNIX* is a powerful operating system. Many servers use the UNIX operating system. ◉ Look up *Linux, operating system,* and *server.*

unzip To *unzip* is to decompress a file or files so that you can use them. Most computers have a program that will unzip a file automatically. ◉ Look up *decompress, file,* and *program.*

up arrow key The *up arrow key* is the key on your keyboard that moves the cursor up by one line. ◉ Look up *cursor* and *keyboard.*

UPC  Look up *universal product code.*

update An *update* is a new version of software or hardware that will replace the existing version of the software or hardware. Look up *software* and *hardware.*

upgrade **(1)** To *upgrade* is to install a newer and better version of a program or hardware. Software upgrades may be available to you for free or at a discounted price if you own a licensed copy of the current version and register your purchase when you buy it.

(2) An *upgrade* is a newer version of software or hardware. Look up *program, software,* and *version number.*

upload When you *upload* a file to another computer, you send the file to the other computer, usually over telephone lines or cable connections using your computer's modem. Look up *download, modem, file,* and *FTP.*

uppercase The capital letters of the alphabet are called *uppercase* letters. For example, A, B, and C are uppercase letters. Look up *lowercase, case insensitive,* and *case sensitive.*

UPS *UPS* is the abbreviation for **U**nited **P**arcel **S**ervice. UPS is a large American carrier of mail order e-tail packages. It can be located on the web at *www.ups.com.* Look up *e-tail.*

upward compatibility When a computer program or accessory works on the machine for which it was designed and on newer models it has *upward compatibility.* Look up *program.*

URL *URL* is an acronym for **u**niform **r**esource **l**ocator. URLs are the addresses that you use to locate information on the Internet. For example, below are the URLs for Apple Computer, Incorporated and

Microsoft. 👁 Look up *acronym, information,* and *Internet.*

> http://www.apple.com
> http://www.microsoft.com

Usenet *Usenet* is a collection of newsgroups available over the Internet. People use Usenet to discuss topics of interest to them. 👁 Look up *Internet.*

user A *user* is a person who uses a computer.

user-friendly A computer or program is *user-friendly* if it is easy to use. 👁 Look up *computer* and *program.*

user group A *user group* is a group of people who come together regularly to learn about some part of the world of computers and the Internet. 👁 Look up *Internet.*

user ID *User ID* stands for user identification. Your user ID is the name that you select to identify yourself to your computer and to the other users of a bulletin board or to an Internet service. Your user ID is not a secret password. 👁 Look up *computer, Internet,* and *password.*

user interface A *user interface* is a computer's way of interacting with the person using it.

user list Computer and software manufacturers collect the names of people who use each of their products. These names are called *user lists*. They usually come from the registration cards that users send to the company that make the product. 👁 Look up *software*.

....

user manual A *user manual* is a book that tells you what you need to know to use a program, a computer, or a device like a mouse or a printer. 👁 Look up *device, mouse, printer,* and *program*.

....

user name A *user name* is a set of letters and symbols that have to be entered to access certain computers or online services. The user name may be a normal name but can be any set of letters and/or symbols. 👁 Look up *online* and *symbol*.

....

utility program A *utility program* is a program that lets you do things that affect how your computer runs. For example, you use utility programs to copy disks, to compress data, or to scan disks and memory for viruses.

How are utility programs different from application programs? Application programs are programs that you use to do something fun or useful that do not have anything to do with how the your computer runs. For example, video games and word-processing programs are application programs. Utility programs, on the other hand, always have something to do with the workings of your computer itself. 👁 Look up *data, data compression, disk, memory, program, scan,* and *virus*.

....

vaccine A *vaccine* is a computer program that protects your computer from viruses by checking the operating system. No vaccine can offer protection from all viruses. 👁 Look up *antivirus program* and *virus*.

vaporware Very often someone promises that software will be created to do such and such, but the software is never made. This is called *vaporware*. 👁 Look up *software*.

VDT *VDT* is the abbreviation for **v**ideo **dis**play **t**erminal. A VDT is a computer monitor. 👁 Look up *monitor*.

VER command MS-DOS systems have version numbers to identify them. The *Ver command* will show the version of MS-DOS your computer is using. Type VER (Enter) at the DOS prompt to display your version. Some programs will not run on some systems, so knowing your version is important. 👁 Look up *DOS, MS-DOS, prompt, program,* and *version number.*

version number Computer programs change often. You may buy Version 3.2 of a program and then see Version 3.3 of the program advertised only a short time later. The company has decided to improve the program in some way.

Why are new versions of software made so often? Computer programs are complicated. There is almost always some way to improve a program. Programmers may find a way to make a program run better, faster, or do more, or bugs may have to be fixed.

Changes may also be made because of changes in computer hardware. Programmers and the companies that they work for want their programs to run on as many machines as possible. So, when new hardware comes along, a new version of a program must be made. One more reason for new versions is the advance of the Internet. The Internet has grown and changed quickly, and programs related to the Internet have changed to keep up.

Look up *hardware, Internet, program,* and *programmer.*

vertical scrolling When you are looking at an image that is too big to fit into a window, you can use scrolling to see all of the image. *Vertical scrolling* means moving the image up and down. Usually, this is done by using the slide bar at the side of the window or by using the vertical wheel on your mouse if you have a mouse with a scrolling wheel. **Look up** *horizontal scrolling, image, mouse, scroll, scrolling wheel,* and *window.*

VGA monitor VGA is an abbreviation for video graphics array. A *VGA monitor* uses analog signals. **Look up** *analog signal.*

video card A *video card* is a plug-in circuit board that makes it possible for a computer to display material on a specific type of monitor. **Look up** *circuit board.*

video clip A *video clip* is a short movie. Many web pages have video clips that you can download and watch. **Look up** *download* and *web page.*

video game   A *video game* is a game that you play using your computer.

virtual reality   *Virtual* means almost. *Reality* means something that exists. *Virtual reality*, then, means almost real. Any program that can make sounds and images that seem almost real is creating virtual reality. Virtual reality is used in everything from airplane pilot training to video games. 👁 Look up *image* and *program.*

virus   An unwanted program that enters your computer from outside is a *virus.* A virus can duplicate itself and then infect your programs and files. Some viruses use all of your memory and shut down your computer. You can buy antivirus programs to protect your computer from most viruses. 👁 Look up *anti-virus program, file, memory,* and *program.*

visited link   A *visited link* on a web site is a link that you have already displayed on your screen. Visited links are usually colored purple to show that they have been visited. 👁 Look up *hyperlink, screen,* and *web site.*

voice mail   *Voice mail* is a message-recording system that is computer controlled. Messages are recorded and played automatically when requested by the recipient.

voice recognition *Voice recognition* is the ability of a device to identify words that you say. If a computer has voice recognition, you can speak to it and your words will be identified, just as they are if you type them.  Look up *device.*

volatile memory *Volatile memory* is memory that stores information until the computer is turned off.  Look up *information* and *memory.*

VR *VR* is an abbreviation for virtual reality.  Look up *virtual reality.*

VRML *VRML* is an abbreviation for virtual reality modeling language. VRML is a scripting language that lets programmers write web pages with 3-D characteristics. The work is then accessible on the Internet.  Look up *Internet* and *programmer.*

W3C *W3C* is an abbreviation for **W**orld **W**ide **W**eb **C**onsortium. 👁 Look up *World Wide Web Consortium.*

WAN *WAN* is an acronym for **w**ide-**a**rea **n**etwork. 👁 Look up *wide-area network.*

warm boot To *warm boot* your computer means to restart your computer after it has been turned on and is running. 👁 Look up *boot, cold boot,* and *computer.*

warp To *warp* is to stretch, bend, or distort in some other way. Warping is often used in computer graphics to make interesting effects.

warranty A *warranty* is a promise that a product will work and that the maker will repair or replace the product if you have certain specified problems with it. If the product has problems not listed in the warranty or problems that result from using the product in the wrong way, it may have to be repaired or replaced at the owner's expense.

wav *wav* is an extension that indicates that a file is a WAVE file. 👁 Look up *WAVE.*

WAVE *WAVE* is an audio-file format. Wave files are audio files that you can listen to. Many web sites have wave files that you can download. 👁 Look up *audio, download, file,* and *web site.*

WB *WB* is an abbreviation for "welcome back." It is used in informal e-mail, chat, and Usenet.

> *John: It's been a long summer away from my friends. I'm glad to be back.*
> *Jawan: We missed you at the clubhouse, **wb**.*

See the appendix, pages 189–190, for a complete table of abbreviations. 👁 Look up *chat, e-mail,* and *Usenet.*

web 👁 Look up *World Wide Web*.

web browser 👁 Look up *browser*.

web design *Web design* is the art and craft of making web pages. 👁 Look up *web page*.

web master A *web master* is a person who controls a web site. The web master is responsible for updating the site, controlling links, dealing with complaints and suggestions from users, and many other things that have to do with the operation of the site. 👁 Look up *hyperlink, user,* and *web site*.

web page A *web page* is a file that you can view by using your web browser. 👁 Look up *browser* and *file*.

web site A *web site* is a file or set of files (or the computer system on which the files are stored) that is available for you to view using your browser. 👁 Look up *browser, computer,* and *file*.

weight *Weight* is the boldness or heaviness of a style of type. Some fonts offer different weights such as demibold, bold, and extra bold. 👁 Look up *bold* and *font*.

wide-area network (WAN) A *wide-area network* is a group of connected computers far away from each other. The Internet is a network of connected WANs. 👁 Look up *Internet, local-area network,* and *tiny-area network*.

widow When the first line of a page is the final line of a paragraph, the line is called a *widow*. Widows should be avoided when you are writing because they are unattractive, and your reader may not see them. Many word processors are programmed to eliminate widows automatically by adjusting the line break. 👁 Look up *orphan, program,* and *word processor.*

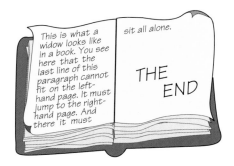

This is what a widow looks like in a book. You see here that the last line of this paragraph cannot fit on the left-hand page. It must jump to the right-hand page. And there it must

sit all alone.

THE END

wild card A *wild card* is a symbol that you use to stand for a letter or letters that you are unsure of in a file name. In DOS and Microsoft Windows, you can use an asterisk (*) for multiple letters, and you can use the question mark (?) for a single letter. For example, games*.exe is used to find all files that begin with games and end with .exe. 👁 Look up *DOS, file, Microsoft Windows,* and *symbol.*

window A *window* is an area of the screen in which a program runs. A window's size can be changed and usually has scroll bars. 👁 Look up *program, screen,* and *scroll bar.*

Windows 👁 Look up *Microsoft Windows.*

wireless communication *Wireless communication* is the transfer of electromagnetic signals from one place to another without the use of cables. The transfer is usually accomplished using infrared light or radio waves.

W/O *W/O* is an abbreviation for "without." It is used in informal e-mail, chat, and Usenet.

> *John: I can't go one day w/o playing video games.*
> *Paul: Me neither. I play for hours.*

See the appendix, pages 189–190, for a complete table of abbreviations. 👁 Look up *chat, e-mail,* and *Usenet.*

WordPerfect *WordPerfect* is a widely used word processing program that can be used on both IBM PC-compatible and Macintosh computers. 👁 Look up *IBM compatible, Macintosh,* and *program.*

word processing *Word processing* means using a computer to make written documents. 👁 Look up *computer.*

word processor A *word processor* is a program that lets you write letters, reports, and so on using a computer.  Look up *computer* and *program*.

word spacing The spacing between words is known as *word spacing*. Look up *interword spacing, letterspacing,* and *tracking.*

word wrap When you type past the end of a line, the cursor jumps to the next line. At the same time, the program arranges the words so that they are not broken at the end of the line. This function is called *word wrap*. Look up *cursor* and *program.*

World Wide Web (WWW) The Internet is a network of computer networks. The *World Wide Web*, on the other hand, is a hypertext system that uses the Internet. In a hypertext system, you can use hyperlinks by clicking to display documents that contain information, graphics, and other hyperlinks.

What is the difference between the Internet and the World Wide Web? The Internet is made of computers and connections. The World Wide Web, on the other hand, is a collection of hypertext documents stored on servers.

👁 Look up *click, graphics, hyperlink, hypertext, information, Internet, network,* and *server.*

World Wide Web Consortium (W3C)

The *World Wide Web Consortium* is a group of organizations that develop standards for the World Wide Web. Without standards, the World Wide Web would not be possible because computers would not be able to communicate with each other, just as people who speak different languages cannot communicate with each other. 👁 Look up *World Wide Web.*

Wozniak, Stephen (Gary) (1950–)

Stephen Wozniak is the founder of Apple Computer, Incorporated, along with Steve Jobs. His nickname is "The Woz."

---

write

To *write* is to record data to a disk. For example, when you save a file to, say, a hard drive, the hard disk drive writes the data onto the hard disk. 👁 Look up *data, disk, file,* and *hard drive.*

---

write-protect

Sometimes you may have something important saved on a diskette. If you want to make sure that it is not changed or copied over, you can *write-protect* the diskette. To write-protect a 3½-inch diskette, you slide the small block at the corner of the disk up so that the opening is uncovered. To write-protect a 5¼-inch disk, you cover the notch with an adhesive strip that comes with the disk. 👁 Look up *diskette.*

NOT WRITE PROTECTED

WRITE PROTECTED

WRITE PROTECTED

NOT WRITE PROTECTED

WRT *WRT* is an abbreviation for "with regard to" or "with respect to." It is used in informal e-mail, chat, and Usenet. See the appendix, pages 189–190, for a complete table of abbreviations. 👁 Look up *chat, e-mail,* and *Usenet.*

WTB *WTB* is an abbreviation for "want to buy." It is used in informal e-mail, chat, and Usenet. See the appendix, pages 189–190, for a complete table of abbreviations. 👁 Look up *chat, e-mail,* and *Usenet.*

WWW *WWW* is an abbreviation for World Wide Web. 👁 Look up *World Wide Web.*

WYSIWYG (pronounced "wizzy wig") *WYSIWYG* is an acronym for **w**hat **y**ou **s**ee **i**s **w**hat **y**ou **g**et. If a word processor or desktop publishing program is WYSIWIG, then when you print a file, the printout will look exactly like what you see on your monitor. 👁 Look up *desktop publishing, file, monitor, print, program,* and *word processor.*

---

x-axis The *x-axis* is the horizontal axis of a graph or of a graphics image. 👁 Look up *y-axis* and *z-axis.*

x-height The *x-height* of a font is the height of the letter *x* or any of the other lowercase letters that do not have ascenders or descenders. 👁 Look up *ascender, lowercase,* and *point.*

Y2K As the year 2000 neared, many people thought that computers would have problems because computers had not been programmed to deal with years beginning with anything other than 19, like the year 2000. People called this the year 2000 problem, or *Y2K* for short. Some people believed that problems would occur with bank computers, military computers, and other impor-

tant computer systems. It turned out that no major problems occurred. 👁 Look up *computer* and *program.*

y-axis The *y-axis* is the vertical axis of a graph or of a graphics image. 👁 Look up *x-axis* and *z-axis.*

YIAH *YIAH* is an abbreviation for "yes, I am here." It is used in informal e-mail, chat, and Usenet.

> John: Hello. Is anyone there?
> Juan: **yiah**. I just got online. I was outside playing.

See the appendix, pages 189–190, for a complete table of abbreviations. 👁 Look up *chat, e-mail,* and *Usenet.*

YMMV *YMMV* is an abbreviation for "your mileage may vary" (your results may be very different from mine). It is used in informal e-mail, chat, and Usenet. See the appendix, pages 189–190, for a complete table of abbreviations. 👁 Look up *chat, e-mail,* and *Usenet.*

yotta- *yotta-* is a prefix that means 1,000,000,000,000,000,000,000,000 (which equals 10^{24}). 👁 Look up *prefix.*

z-axis The *z-axis* is most often the axis that appears to jut out into space from the computer screen or a page. The z-axis is important in 3-D graphics because 3-D graphics create an image that seems to come out at you when you look at it. When programmers or artists make such images, they use the z-axis to control the depth of parts of the image, which is what gives the 3-D effect. 👁 Look up *3-D rendering, computer screen,* and *image.*

zoom in To *zoom in* on something means to enlarge its image so that you can see fine details. As the fine details become larger, the field of vision becomes smaller. 👁 Look up *image.*

Zip disk A *Zip disk* is a kind of disk on which your computer can store information. Zip disks can store 100 megabytes of information, which is about 69 times as much information as a 1.44-megabyte 3½-inch diskette. 👁 Look up *3½-inch diskette, computer,* and *megabyte.*

zoom out To *zoom out* means to shrink all of the parts of an image so that you can see the big picture. 👁 Look up *image.*

Zip drive A *Zip drive* is a disk drive that uses Zip disks. 👁 Look up *disk drive* and *Zip disk.*

ZIP file A *ZIP file* is a file that has been compressed using the PKZIP algorithm. ZIP files end in .zip. 👁 Look up *data compression.*

APPENDIX

Table of Abbreviations Used in E-mail, Chat, and Usenet

he abbreviations in this table are only to be used in informal communication. Do not use them, for example, if you are writing a school report.

Abbreviation	Meaning	Abbreviation	Meaning
AAMOF	"as a matter of fact"	FWIW	"for what it is worth"
AFAIK	"as far as I know"	FYI	"for your information"
AFAIR	"as far as I remember"	G2G	"got to go"
AFK	"away from keyboard"	GFETE	"grinning from ear to ear"
AYT	"are you there?"		
BAK	"back at keyboard"	GG	"gotta' go"
BBIAF	"be back in a few minutes"	GMTA	"great minds think alike"
BBL	"be back later"	GTG	"got to go"
BRB	"be right back"	HTH	"hope this helps"
BTDT	"been there, done that"	IANAL	"I am not a lawyer"
BTW	"by the way"	ICCL	"I could not care less"
CUL8R	"see you later"	IIRC	"if I remember correctly"
CYA	"see ya"		
DIIK	"darned if I know"	IM	"instant message"
DIKU	"do I know you?"	IMHO	"in my humble opinion"
DTS	"don't think so"	IMO	"in my opinion"
EG	"evil grin"	IOW	"in other words"
F2F	"face to face"	IRL	"in real life"

Abbreviation	Meaning	Abbreviation	Meaning
ISO	"in search of"	RYFM	"read your friendly manual"
K	"OK"		
LOL	"laughing out loud"	TIA	"thanks in advance"
LTNS	"long time no see"	TLA	"three-letter abbreviation"
NP	"no problem"		
OBO	"or best offer"	TNX	"thanks"
OIC	"oh, I see"	TTFN	"ta ta for now"
OTOH	"on the other hand"	TTYL	"talk to you later"
PPL	"people"	UGTBK	"you have got to be kidding"
RE	"regards"		
ROFL	"rolling on the floor laughing"	WB	"welcome back"
		W/O	"without"
ROTFL	"rolling on the floor laughing"	WRT	"with regard to" or "with respect to"
		WTB	"want to buy"
RSN	"real soon now"	YIAH	"yes, I am here"
RTFM	"read the friendly manual"	YMMV	"your mileage may vary" (your results may be very different from mine)
RUMOF	"are you male or female?"		

Table of Binary & Hexadecimal Numbers from 0 through 255

 ere are the numbers 0 through 255 and their binary and hexadecimal equivalents. These values are used in programming, Web design, and other purposes.

Dec	Bin	Hex	Dec	Bin	Hex
0	0	00	32	100000	20
1	1	01	33	100001	21
2	10	02	34	100010	22
3	11	03	35	100011	23
4	100	04	36	100100	24
5	101	05	37	100101	25
6	110	06	38	100110	26
7	111	07	39	100111	27
8	1000	08	40	101000	28
9	1001	09	41	101001	29
10	1010	0A	42	101010	2A
11	1011	0B	43	101011	2B
12	1100	0C	44	101100	2C
13	1101	0D	45	101101	2D
14	1110	0E	46	101110	2E
15	1111	0F	47	101111	2F
16	10000	10	48	110000	30
17	10001	11	49	110001	31
18	10010	12	50	110010	32
19	10011	13	51	110011	33
20	10100	14	52	110100	34
21	10101	15	53	110101	35
22	10110	16	54	110110	36
23	10111	17	55	110111	37
24	11000	18	56	111000	38
25	11001	19	57	111001	39
26	11010	1A	58	111010	3A
27	11011	1B	59	111011	3B
28	11100	1C	60	111100	3C
29	11101	1D	61	111101	3D
30	11110	1E	62	111110	3E
31	11111	1F	63	111111	3F

Table of Binary & Hexadecimal Numbers from 0 through 255 (continued)

Dec	Bin	Hex	Dec	Bin	Hex
64	1000000	40	96	1100000	60
65	1000001	41	97	1100001	61
66	1000010	42	98	1100010	62
67	1000011	43	99	1100011	63
68	1000100	44	100	1100100	64
69	1000101	45	101	1100101	65
70	1000110	46	102	1100110	66
71	1000111	47	103	1100111	67
72	1001000	48	104	1101000	68
73	1001001	49	105	1101001	69
74	1001010	4A	106	1101010	6A
75	1001011	4B	107	1101011	6B
76	1001100	4C	108	1101100	6C
77	1001101	4D	109	1101101	6D
78	1001110	4E	110	1101110	6E
79	1001111	4F	111	1101111	6F
80	1010000	50	112	1110000	70
81	1010001	51	113	1110001	71
82	1010010	52	114	1110010	72
83	1010011	53	115	1110011	73
84	1010100	54	116	1110100	74
85	1010101	55	117	1110101	75
86	1010110	56	118	1110110	76
87	1010111	57	119	1110111	77
88	1011000	58	120	1111000	78
89	1011001	59	121	1111001	79
90	1011010	5A	122	1111010	7A
91	1011011	5B	123	1111011	7B
92	1011100	5C	124	1111100	7C
93	1011101	5D	125	1111101	7D
94	1011110	5E	126	1111110	7E
95	1011111	5F	127	1111111	7F

Table of Binary & Hexadecimal Numbers from 0 through 255

Dec	Bin	Hex	Dec	Bin	Hex
128	10000000	80	160	10100000	A0
129	10000001	81	161	10100001	A1
130	10000010	82	162	10100010	A2
131	10000011	83	163	10100011	A3
132	10000100	84	164	10100100	A4
133	10000101	85	165	10100101	A5
134	10000110	86	166	10100110	A6
135	10000111	87	167	10100111	A7
136	10001000	88	168	10101000	A8
137	10001001	89	169	10101001	A9
138	10001010	8A	170	10101010	AA
139	10001011	8B	171	10101011	AB
140	10001100	8C	172	10101100	AC
141	10001101	8D	173	10101101	AD
142	10001110	8E	174	10101110	AE
143	10001111	8F	175	10101111	AF
144	10010000	90	176	10110000	B0
145	10010001	91	177	10110001	B1
146	10010010	92	178	10110010	B2
147	10010011	93	179	10110011	B3
148	10010100	94	180	10110100	B4
149	10010101	95	181	10110101	B5
150	10010110	96	182	10110110	B6
151	10010111	97	183	10110111	B7
152	10011000	98	184	10111000	B8
153	10011001	99	185	10111001	B9
154	10011010	9A	186	10111010	BA
155	10011011	9B	187	10111011	BB
156	10011100	9C	188	10111100	BC
157	10011101	9D	189	10111101	BD
158	10011110	9E	190	10111110	BE
159	10011111	9F	191	10111111	BF

Table of Binary & Hexadecimal Numbers from 0 through 255 (continued)

Dec	Bin	Hex	Dec	Bin	Hex
192	11000000	C0	224	11100000	E0
193	11000001	C1	225	11100001	E1
194	11000010	C2	226	11100010	E2
195	11000011	C3	227	11100011	E3
196	11000100	C4	228	11100100	E4
197	11000101	C5	229	11100101	E5
198	11000110	C6	230	11100110	E6
199	11000111	C7	231	11100111	E7
200	11001000	C8	232	11101000	E8
201	11001001	C9	233	11101001	E9
202	11001010	CA	234	11101010	EA
203	11001011	CB	235	11101011	EB
204	11001100	CC	236	11101100	EC
205	11001101	CD	237	11101101	ED
206	11001110	CE	238	11101110	EE
207	11001111	CF	239	11101111	EF
208	11010000	D0	240	11110000	F0
209	11010001	D1	241	11110001	F1
210	11010010	D2	242	11110010	F2
211	11010011	D3	243	11110011	F3
212	11010100	D4	244	11110100	F4
213	11010101	D5	245	11110101	F5
214	11010110	D6	246	11110110	F6
215	11010111	D7	247	11110111	F7
216	11011000	D8	248	11111000	F8
217	11011001	D9	249	11111001	F9
218	11011010	DA	250	11111010	FA
219	11011011	DB	251	11111011	FB
220	11011100	DC	252	11111100	FC
221	11011101	DD	253	11111101	FD
222	11011110	DE	254	11111110	FE
223	11011111	DF	255	11111111	FF

Country Codes

 hese codes at the end of addresses tell where a computer is located.

Code	Country
au	Australia
ca	Canada
de	Germany
fr	France
nl	Netherlands
se	Sweden
uk	United Kingdom

Organizations

 hese suffixes at the end of an e-mail address or web site show what kind of organization or institution is at the address or site.

Code	Meaning
ac	academic organization
com	commercial organization
edu	educational institution
gov	government body
int	international organization
mil	military organization
net	organization involved in the operations of the Internet
org	nonprofit organization

Suggested Readings

 The following is a selection of books about computers and the Internet.

Aker, Sharon Zardetto. *The Macintosh Bible.* Berkeley: Peachpit Press, 1998.

Ames, Andrea L., David R. Nadeau, and John L. Moreland. *VRML 2.0 Sourcebook,* 2nd edition. New York: John Wiley & Sons, Inc., 1997.

Bach, Maurice J. *The Design of the UNIX Operating System.* Upper Saddle River: Prentice-Hall, 1986.

Cagle, Kurt, et al. *Beginning XML.* Birmingham: Wrox Press Ltd., 2000.

Castro, Elizabeth. *HTML 4 for the World Wide Web,* 4th edition. Berkeley: Peachpit Press, 2000.

Conner-Sax, Kiersten and Krol, ed. *The Whole Internet: The Next Generation.* Sebastopol: O'Reilly, 1999.

Dale, Nell. *C++ Plus Data Structures.* Sudbury: Jones and Bartlett Publishers, 1999.

Davis, Jack and Susan Merritt. *The Web Design Wow! Book.* Berkeley: Peachpit Press, 1998.

Deftler, Frank J., Jr., and Les Freed. *How Networks Work,* 4th edition. Indianapolis: Que, 1998.

Downing, Douglas A., et al. *Dictionary of Computer and Internet Terms,* 7th edition. Hauppauge: Barron's Educational Series, Inc., 1998.

Flanagan, David. *Java in a Nutshell,* 2nd edition. Sebastopol: O'Reilly, 1997.

Floyd, Michael. *Building Web Sites with XML.* Upper Saddle River: Prentice Hall PTR, 2000.

Garfinkel, Simson and Gene Spafford. *Pratical UNIX & Internet Security.* Sebastopol: O'Reilly, 1996.

Glossbrenner, Alfred and Emily Glossbrenner. *Search Engines for the World Wide Web,* 2nd edition. Berkeley: Peachpit Press, 1999.

Goodman, Danny. *Dynamic HTML: The Definitive Reference.* Sebastopol: O'Reilly, 1998.

Grimes, Galen. *10 Minute Guide to the Internet and the World Wide Web.* Indianapolis: Que, 1997.

Hafner, Katie and Matthew Lyon. *Where Wizards Stay Up Late: The Origins of the Internet.* Simon & Schuster, 1997.

Hekman, Jessica P. *Linux in a Nutshell.* Sebastopol: O'Reilly, 1997.

Hergett, Douglas. *How to Use Windows 98.* Indianapolis: Sams Publishing, 1998.

Kernighan, Brian W. and Dennis M. Ritchie. *The C Programming Language,* 2nd edition. Prentice Hall, 1988.

Kernighan, Brian W. and Rob Pike. *The Practice of Programming.* Reading: Addison-Wesley, 1999.

Maran, Ruth. *Computers Simplified,* 4th edition. Foster City: IDG Books Worldwide, Inc., 1998.

———. *Teach Yourself Computers and the Internet Visually,* 2nd edition. Foster City: IDG Books Worldwide, Inc., 1998.

———. *Windows 95 Simplified.* Foster City: IDG Books Worldwide, Inc., 1995.

———. *Windows 98 Simplified.* Foster City: IDG Books Worldwide, Inc., 1998.

Marchal, Benoît. *XML by Example.* Indianapolis: Que, 2000.

McDonnell, Sharon. *The Everything Internet Book.* Holbrook: Adams Media Corporations, 1999.

Microsoft Windows 98 Step by Step. Redmond: Microsoft Press, 1998.

Musciano, Chuck and Bill Kennedy. *HTML: The Definitive Guide,* 3rd edition. Sebastopol: O'Reilly, 1998.

Negrino, Tom and Dori Smith. *JavaScript for the World Wide Web,* 3rd edition. Berkeley: Peachpit Press, 1999.

Nelson, Stephen L. *Smart Guide to the Internet.* New York: Barnes & Noble Books, 1999.

———. *Smart Guide to Personal Computers.* Westbury: Barnes & Noble, Inc., 1999.

———. *Smart Guide to Windows 98.* Westbury: Barnes & Noble, Inc., 1998.

Niederst, Jennifer. *Web Design in a Nutshell.* Sebastopol: O'Reilly, 1999.

O'Reilly, Tim, Troy Mott, and Walter Glenn. *Windows 98 in a Nutshell.* Sebastopol: O'Reilly, 1999.

Oualline, Steven. *Practical C Programming.* Sebastopol: O'Reilly, 1993.

Polly, Armour. *The Internet & Family Yellow Pages,* 2nd edition. Berkeley: Osborne/McGraw-Hill, 1997.

Powell, Thomas A. *Web Design: The Complete Reference.* Berkeley: Osborne/McGraw-Hill, 2000.

Schildt, Herbert. *Teach Yourself C,* 3rd edition. Berkeley: Osborne/McGraw-Hill, 1997.

Sherman, Aliza. *Cybergrrl! A Woman's Guide to the World Wide Web.* New York: Ballentine: 1998.

Siever, Ellen, Stephen Spainhour, and Nathan Patwardhan. *Perl in a Nutshell.* Sebastopol: O'Reilly, 1999.

Stern, Judith and Robert Lettier. *Quicktime and Movieplayer Pro 3.* Berkeley: Peachpit Press, 1998.

Williams, Robin. *The iMac Book,* 2nd edition. Berkeley: Peachpit Press, 2000.

Wing, Kelleigh, Paul Whitehead, and Ruth Maran. *Internet and World Wide Web Simplified,* 3rd edition. Foster City: IDG Books Worldwide, Inc., 1999.

———. *Teach Yourself Internet and World Wide Web Visually,* 2nd edition. Foster City: IDG Books Worldwide, Inc. 1999.

Wingate, Philippa and Asha Kalbag. *The Osborne Complete Book of Internet & World Wide Web.* Tulsa: EDC Publishing, 1999.

Wolff, Michael. *Net Guide: Your Complete Guide to the Internet and Online Service.* Round Rock, TX: Dell, 1997.

Young, Michael J. *Step by Step XML.* Redmond: Microsoft Press, 2000.

Table of Metric Prefixes

 etric prefixes are used to show multiplication or division by units of ten.

Prefix		Meaning
yotta-		multiply by 1,000,000,000,000,000,000,000,000
zetta-		multiply by 1,000,000,000,000,000,000,000 000
exa-		multiply by 1,000,000,000,000,000,000
peta-		multiply by 1,000,000,000,000,000
tera-	(T)	multiply by 1,000,000,000,000 (1,099,511,627,776 in computer usage)
giga-	(G)	multiply by 1,000,000,000 (1,073,741,824 in computer usage)
mega-	(M)	multiply by 1,000,000 (1,048,576 in computer usage)
kilo-	(k)	multiply by 1000 (1024 in computer usage)
hecta-		multiply by 100
deca-		multiply by 10
deci-	(d)	divide by 10
centi-	(c)	divide by 100
milli-	(m)	divide by 1000
micro-	(µ)	divide by 1,000,000
nano-	(n)	divide by 1,000,000,000
pico-	(p)	divide by 1,000,000,000,000
femto-	(f)	divide by 1,000,000,000,000,000
atto-	(a)	divide by 1,000,000,000,000,000,000

Thickness Measurements

 oint sizes are used in graphics, word processing, web design, and many other applications. Below, each line has the given thickness.

¼ point

½ point

¾ point

1 point

1½ point

2¼ point

3 point

4½ point

6 point

7 point

8 point

9 point

10 point

11 point

12 point

14 point

16 point

18 point

24 point

36 point

48 point

60 point

72 point

Table of Font Types

ifferent font types are used to create various types of documents.

Helvetica	This is an example of text in Helvetica Numbers in Helvetica: 0, 1, 2, 3, 4, 5, 6, 7, 8, 9 Symbols in Helvetica: ~ ! @ # $ % ^ & * < > ? / {
Century Old Style	This is an example of text in Century Old Style Numbers in Century Old Style: 0, 1, 2, 3, 4, 5, 6, 7, 8, 9 Symbols in Century Old Style: ~ ! @ # $ % ^ & * < > ? / {
Futura	This is an example of text in Futura Numbers in Futura: 0, 1, 2, 3, 4, 5, 6, 7, 8, 9 Symbols in Futura: ~ ! @ # $ % ^ & * < > ? / {
Stone Informal	This is an example of text in Stone Informal Numbers in Stone Informal: 0, 1, 2, 3, 4, 5, 6, 7, 8, 9 Symbols in Stone Informal: ~ ! @ # $ % ^ & * < > ? / {
Franklin Gothic	This is an example of text in Franklin Gothic Numbers in Franklin Gothic: 0, 1, 2, 3, 4, 5, 6, 7, 8, 9 Symbols in Franklin Gothic: ~ ! @ # $ % ^ & * < > ? / {
Lubalin Graph	This is an example of text in Lubalin Graph Numbers in Lubalin Graph: 0, 1, 2, 3, 4, 5, 6, 7, 8, 9 Symbols in Lubalin Graph: ~ ! @ # $ % ^ & * < > ? / {
Optima	This is an example of text in Optima Numbers in Optima: 0, 1, 2, 3, 4, 5, 6, 7, 8, 9 Symbols in Optima: ~ ! @ # $ % ^ & * < > ? / {
Bookman	This is an example of text in Bookman Numbers in Bookman: 0, 1, 2, 3, 4, 5, 6, 7, 8, 9 Symbols in Bookman: ~ ! @ # $ % ^ & * < > ? / {

GAMES

GAME 1
Computer & Internet Word Search

Find each term related to computers and the Internet.

```
Z  I  P  D  R  I  V  E  P  R  O  G  R  A  M
R  E  L  B  C  C  P  U  J  Y  N  Q  S  K  O
D  L  A  P  T  O  P  R  P  N  L  I  M  Y  U
I  A  U  O  E  M  T  K  I  Z  I  S  O  C  S
S  N  F  R  N  V  S  U  M  I  N  V  D  O  E
K  F  L  T  O  I  S  P  W  M  E  D  E  I  R
E  C  A  R  D  L  I  M  O  Q  W  M  M  N  E
T  V  R  D  B  O  R  S  D  A  T  A  T  I  M
T  O  R  G  W  G  T  B  N  X  C  F  T  G  E
E  A  W  X  W  E  B  S  I  T  E  R  W  A  N
H  P  T  E  W  B  I  J  W  E  G  M  N  M  U
```

AI	data	LAN	mouse	port	window
card	diskette	laptop	net	program	WWW
com	hard disk	~~menu~~	online	WAN	ZIP drive
CPU	ISP	modem	org	web site	

Answers appear on page 226.

GAME 2
Programming Word Search

Find each term related to programming.

```
G  N  I  T  S  E  T  A  H  P  L  A  L  P  H
N  L  U  O  B  A  S  I  C  A  S  I  A  O  L
I  A  Y  R  U  D  A  S  +  +  B  C  N  P  D
T  M  U  T  E  D  I  N  A  R  C  U  G  R  D
S  I  N  S  T  R  U  C  T  I  O  N  U  O  R
E  C  C  E  X  E  C  U  T  E  M  O  A  G  E
T  E  I  C  +  S  Y  T  E  E  P  B  G  R  J
A  D  S  +  S  S  Y  T  M  E  I  M  E  A  M
T  A  C  O  D  E  B  O  X  T  L  S  V  M  M
E  X  L  E  R  T  R  X  M  X  E  A  X  M  E
B  E  M  P  I  Y  L  A  A  R  R  A  S  E  R
H  H  E  X  D  B  P  I  C  B  I  N  A  R  Y
```

address	~~byte~~	instruction
alpha testing	C++	Java
BASIC	code	language
beta testing	compiler	memory
binary	execute	programmer
bitmap	hexadecimal	run

Answers appear on page 226.

GAME 3
Graphic Terms Word Search

Find each term related to graphics.

```
F   O   R   E   S   O   L   U   T   I   O   N   E   I
D   M   O   N   O   C   H   R   O   M   E   R   A   M
R   C   M   Y   K   R   O   G   R   A   M   M   R   P
E   G   Z   A   X   I   S   B   X   E   L   X   A   B
N   X   N   X   N   I   T   C   R   P   M   I   Y   Y
D   A   T   I   S   O   L   O   A   I   N   A   T   H
E   X   A   S   X   I   E   L   S   T   R   S   A   P
R   I   Q   X   M   X   E   O   P   R   H   N   S   I
I   S   X   A   X   T   S   R   A   W   D   H   J   X
N   R   G   P   T   C   O   S   K   L   R   P   C   E
G   E   R   E   G   G   G   B   E   J   R   R   Q   L
H   K   Q   S   R   I   X   V   E   C   T   O   R   I
R   D   R   A   W   P   R   O   G   R   A   M   Q   S
Q   J   M   O   N   I   T   O   R   M   M   Y   K   L
```

array	monochrome	resolution
cmyk	morph	~~RGB color~~
draw program	paint program	vector
handle	palette	x-axis
image	pixel	y-axis
monitor	rendering	z-axis

Answers appear on page 226.

GAME 4
Computer Troubles Word Search

Find each term related to computer problems.

```
I  O  C  R  A  S  H  R  E  K  C  A  R  C  L
N  M  B  R  C  K  E  A  Q  V  U  R  G  E  I
F  S  M  A  L  F  U  N  C  T  I  O  N  P  N
E  R  E  S  U  N  C  T  W  K  F  R  B  R  E
C  V  E  C  R  D  O  O  T  O  E  R  U  E  S
T  G  R  B  U  N  E  E  B  U  D  R  R  S  U
E  J  M  P  O  R  L  B  R  E  B  W  O  T  R
D  O  B  U  G  O  I  U  U  R  A  S  D  A  G
B  U  R  B  E  Q  T  T  G  G  R  O  R  R  E
E  M  A  R  G  O  R  P  Y  T  I  L  I  T  U
E  T  R  O  J  A  N  H  O  R  S  E  E  M  M
```

bomb
cracker
crash
debug
down
error

hacker
infected
line surge
malfunction
~~reboot~~
restart

security
Trojan horse
utility program
virus

Answers appear on page 226.

GAME 5
Surfing the Net Word Search

Find each term related to surfing the Internet.

```
H  T  M  Q  F  T  C  O  O  K  I  E  E  A
H  I  T  H  E  N  E  T  F  O  R  G  I  R
T  B  I  F  E  O  U  I  O  K  O  D  I  E
M  A  R  E  E  H  C  A  C  A  E  O  E  F
L  U  J  O  I  O  E  A  L  E  S  W  E  R
S  P  P  A  W  E  B  S  I  T  E  N  C  E
C  T  E  A  O  S  A  Y  N  J  R  L  L  S
L  T  G  M  L  E  E  E  K  A  V  O  I  H
I  H  S  E  R  V  E  R  O  V  E  A  E  T
N  O  O  H  I  F  O  R  W  A  R  D  N  F
N  U  P  L  O  A  D  I  J  A  V  D  T  U
I  N  T  E  R  N  E  T  I  O  U  P  U  O
```

Back	Forward	Internet	surf
browser	FTP	Java	The Net
cache	GIF	JPEG	upload
client	hit	~~link~~	web site
cookie	HTML	refresh	
download	http	server	

Answers appear on page 227.

GAME 6
Acronyms & Abbreviations Word Search

Find each acronym or abbreviation.

```
W  U  T  T  P  K  G  I  G  O  H  T  T  P
G  M  D  P  W  K  U  W  C  P  J  Q  T  R
P  E  R  L  W  A  Q  R  A  Q  P  F  Q  I
T  M  L  P  T  P  N  F  L  A  N  C  S  W
H  B  G  M  P  W  A  P  W  A  S  C  R  T
M  R  A  D  T  S  T  W  V  I  S  T  M  L
Y  R  W  S  Q  H  V  I  M  Q  B  C  Q  Z
K  M  P  D  I  S  D  M  F  T  T  M  I  M
W  F  H  U  Q  C  Q  P  A  F  M  Y  Q  I
W  Q  G  Q  P  H  E  E  I  H  C  K  W  F
H  T  T  U  J  P  E  G  T  T  P  W  R  T
B  A  S  F  F  W  S  I  B  P  W  E  G  T
```

ASCII	FPS	IBM	RAM
AVI	FTP	IP	SCSI
BASIC	GIF	JPEG	TIFF
Cc	GIGO	LAN	URL
CMYK	GUI	MPEG	WAN
CPU	HTML	OCR	WWW
~~CRT~~	HTTP	Perl	

Answers appear on page 227.

GAME 7
Abbreviations in Informal E-Mail, Chat, and Usenet Word Search

Find each abbreviation.

C	U	L	8	R	C	Y	D	G	D	T	S	T	A
T	S	2	F	O	G	E	T	P	T	Q	F	C	L
F	2	T	T	F	N	X	P	K	Q	W	N	2	K
U	J	U	E	L	O	L	B	B	I	W	Q	J	F
G	W	T	T	O	I	C	8	W	2	Y	Q	O	L
T	E	C	F	Y	Q	C	Y	A	F	I	M	T	B
I	C	Q	A	F	A	I	R	P	P	A	G	R	C
A	F	A	I	K	2	R	A	Y	A	H	B	8	K
O	F	N	B	B	X	C	M	T	C	8	L	B	Y
K	H	8	B	V	R	P	D	C	M	G	T	Q	2
R	U	M	S	I	S	T	Z	G	2	G	N	N	K
C	E	2	I	R	B	C	C	I	U	O	S	K	X

AAMOF (as a matter of fact)
AFAIK (as far as I know)
AFAIR (as far as I remember)
AFK (away from keyboard)
AYT (Are you there?)
BBIAF (be back in a few minutes)
BBL (be back later)
BRB (be right back)
BTDT (been there, done that)
CUL8R (see you later)
CYA (See ya.)
DTS (Don't think so.)
F2F (face to face)
FWIW (for what it's worth)
G2G (Got to go.)
GFETE (grinning from ear to ear)

GMTA (great minds think alike)
ICCL (I couldn't care less.)
IIRC (if I remember correctly)
IMHO (in my humble opinion)
LOL (laughing out loud)
LTNS (Long time no see.)
OIC (Oh, I see.)
PPL (people)
RE (regards)
ROFL (rolling on the floor laughing)
TIA (thanks in advance)
TNX (thanks)
TTFN (Ta ta for now.)
UGTBK (You've got to be kidding.)
WB (Welcome back.)
YIAH (Yes, I am here.)

Answers appear on page 227.

GAME 8
Using a Computer Word Search

Find each term related to using a computer.

```
E  Z  I  M  Q  A  N  Z  E  L  O  M  A  R
C  O  N  N  E  D  O  W  N  L  O  A  D  W
N  O  G  O  L  O  G  O  F  F  E  X  E  D
T  P  P  X  W  P  M  I  N  I  M  I  Z  E
C  R  T  Y  H  E  J  W  E  M  U  M  T  L
E  S  O  L  C  N  E  D  Z  A  W  I  Y  E
N  Z  O  G  N  T  W  K  I  X  M  Z  U  T
N  W  Q  I  U  U  J  L  L  O  P  E  Q  E
O  O  B  C  A  B  L  L  A  T  S  N  I  L
C  P  E  N  L  N  E  X  I  X  L  Z  U  C
M  X  D  X  P  I  N  D  T  L  A  R  L  E
E  U  N  C  H  R  C  T  I  E  X  E  V  V
D  D  A  O  L  P  U  K  N  T  A  V  O  S
C  U  I  A  V  E  P  R  I  N  T  A  E  L
A  L  L  T  O  O  B  M  I  N  D  S  A  L
```

boot
clean (an infected disk)
click
close
connect
copy (a file)
debug (a program)
delete

download
edit
execute
initialize (a disk)
install
kill (a program)
launch
log off

log on
maximize (a window)
minimize (a window)
open
print
save (a file)
upload

Answers appear on page 227.

GAME 9
Graphic Terms Word Scramble

Unscramble each term related to graphics.

1. IXPEL   1. __ __ __ __ __

2. TOCVER   2. __ __ __ __ __ __

3. TIONRESLUO   3. __ __ __ __ __ __ __ __ __

4. PHMOR   4. __ __ __ __ __

5. AGEIM   5. __ __ __ __ __

6. WARD GRAMPRO   6. __ __ __ __ __ __ __ __ __ __

7. TNIAP GRAMPRO 7. __ __ __ __ __ __ __ __ __ __ __ __

8. RAYAR   8. __ __ __ __ __

9. DLEHANS   9. __ __ __ __ __ __ __

Answers appear on page 228.

GAME 10
Computer Troubles Word Scramble

Unscramble each term related to computer problems.

1. BMOB

1. ___ ___ ___ ___

2. ERHACK

2. ___ ___ ___ ___ ___ ___

3. STARTRE

3. ___ ___ ___ ___ ___ ___ ___

4. RECRACK

4. ___ ___ ___ ___ ___ ___ ___

5. FECTEDIN

5. ___ ___ ___ ___ ___ ___ ___ ___

6. CURITYSE

6. ___ ___ ___ ___ ___ ___ ___ ___

7. HCARS

7. ___ ___ ___ ___ ___

8. LINIE ERUGS

8. ___ ___ ___ ___ ___   ___ ___ ___ ___

9. JANTRO OHRSE

9. ___ ___ ___ ___ ___   ___ ___ ___ ___ ___

10. BUGDE

10. ___ ___ ___ ___ ___

11. FUNCTIONMAL

11. ___ ___ ___ ___ ___ ___ ___ ___ ___ ___ ___

12. TILITYU GRAMPRO

12. ___ ___ ___ ___ ___ ___ ___

___ ___ ___ ___ ___ ___

13. NWOD

13. ___ ___ ___ ___

14. RUSVI

14. ___ ___ ___ ___ ___

15. RORER

15. ___ ___ ___ ___ ___

Answers appear on page 228.

GAME 11
Surfing the Net Word Scramble

Unscramble each term related to surfing the Net.

1. KCAB   1. ___ ___ ___ ___

2. KNIL   2. ___ ___ ___ ___

3. SERBROW   3. ___ ___ ___ ___ ___ ___ ___

4. TIH   4. ___ ___ ___

5. FRESHRE   5. ___ ___ ___ ___ ___ ___ ___

6. EHCAC   6. ___ ___ ___ ___ ___

7. VERSER   7. ___ ___ ___ ___ ___ ___

8. ENTCLI   8. ___ ___ ___ ___ ___ ___

9. FRUS   9. ___ ___ ___ ___

10. IECOOK   10. ___ ___ ___ ___ ___ ___

11. TERINNET   11. ___ ___ ___ ___ ___ ___ ___ ___

12. LOADDWON   12. ___ ___ ___ ___ ___ ___ ___ ___

13. AVAJ   13. ___ ___ ___ ___

14. LOADUP   14. ___ ___ ___ ___ ___ ___

15. BWE IETS   15. ___ ___ ___   ___ ___ ___ ___

Answers appear on page 228.

GAME 12
Computer & Internet Criss Cross

Hint: Word in bold box: MODEM

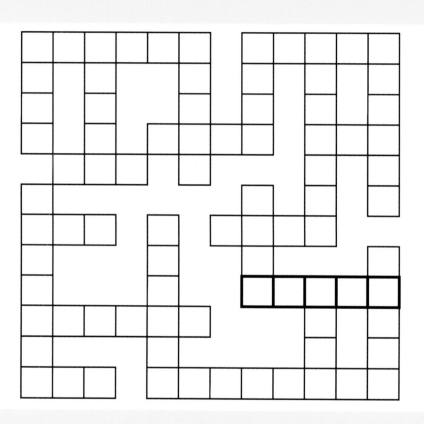

3 letters	4 letters	5 letters	6 letters	7 letters
Esc	data	field	daemon	default
RAM	file	image	format	encrypt
tag	font	modem	laptop	
Web	form	range	update	**8 letters**
	port	toner		pixelate
	text			

Answers appear on page 228.

GAME 13
Computer & Internet Criss Cross

Hint: Word in bold box: OUTPUT

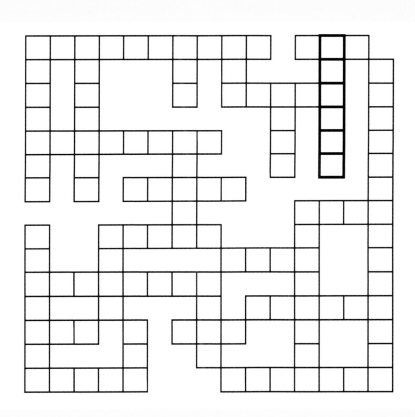

3 letters	**4 letters**	**5 letters**	**6 letters**	android	**10 letters**
bit	byte	crash	scroll	message	simulation
com	chat	debug	output		
GIG	copy	robot		**8 letters**	**14 letters**
OCR	edit	serif	**7 letters**	inactive	virtual reality
org	kill	virus	density	database	
TAN			session	keypress	

Answers appear on page 228.

GAME 14
Binary Madness Criss Cross

Fit each string of 1's and 0's into its proper place in the grid.
Hint: Number in bold box: 1100

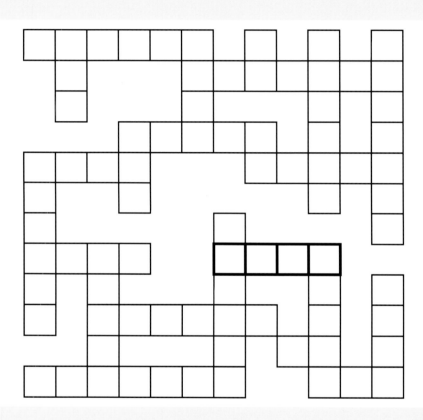

2 digits	3 digits	4 digits	5 digits	6 digits	7 digits
00	000	0011	00100	011011	0011000
01	100	1001	01111	100001	1101111
10	111	1010	10100	101010	1111011
		1011	11110	110101	
		1111		111100	

Answers appear on page 229.

GAME 15
Computer & Internet Criss Cross

Hint: Word in bold box: INTERNET

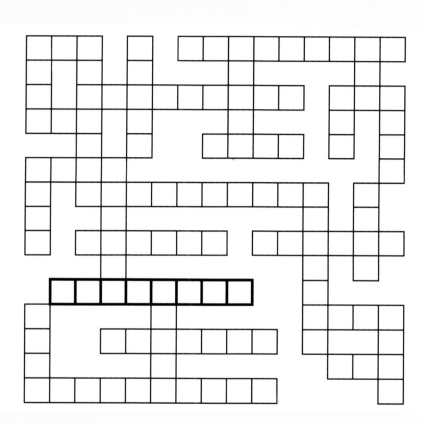

3 letters	**4 letters**	user	**6 letters**	**7 letters**	**9 letters**
FTP	edit	Wave	active	monitor	interface
GIF	font		cookie	network	web design
GIG	GIGO	**5 letters**	reboot	printer	
GUI	menu	board			**10 letters**
LAN	ream	Intel		**8 letters**	nanosecond
TAN	scan	range		Internet	resolution
	UNIX				

Answers appear on page 229.

Games

GAME 16
Computer & Internet Criss Cross

Hint: Word in bold box: DISK

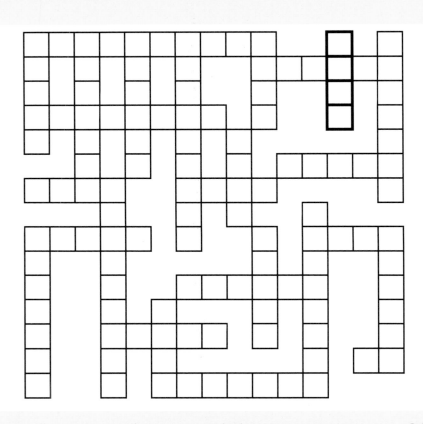

2 letters	edit	alias	device	recover	**9 letters**
IE	host	clean	online	web site	trackball
	port	modem	toggle		scroll bar
4 letters	site	point		**8 letters**	
bomb			**7 letters**	emoticon	**10 letters**
byte	**5 letters**	**6 letters**	acronym	ghosting	mirror site
disk	abort	access	bootleg		

Answers appear on page 229.

GAME 17
Computer & Internet Criss Cross

Hint: Word in bold box: ORIENTATION

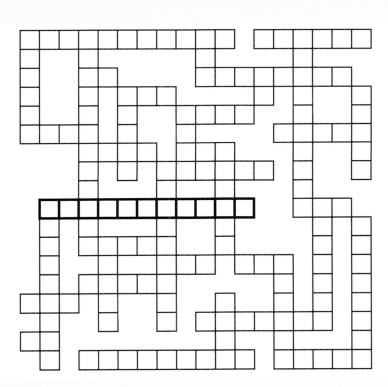

2 letters	fps	port	gamma	reboot	**9 letters**	**11 letters**
AI	GIG	save	mouse	system	character	orientation
IE	hit	text	robot		optimizer	ragged
MB	RAM			**7 letters**	Page Up	right
pt.	ROM	**5 letters**	**6 letters**	offline	key	
		abort	bitmap	palette		**12 letters**
3 letters	**4 letters**	ASCII	client		**10 letters**	gamma
AVI	edit	caddy	memory	**8 letters**	transistor	testing
cpi	perl	field		inactive		
				template		

Answers appear on page 229.

Games

GAME 18
Computer & Internet Word Match

Match each description to the correct term.

1. John used a _____ to write a letter to his grandmother.

2. Jane sent John an _____ telling him about the party.

3. Tom wanted to learn more about the GalaxyMagic video game company, so he went to their _____ on the World Wide Web.

4. My computer crashed. I hope that I did not lose any _____ .

5. To see more of a document, use the _____ .

6. A(n) _____ is a wild card.

7. Click the _____ to begin the game.

8. A(n) _____ is a kind of movie file.

9. An image on a computer screen is made up of _____ .

10. A _____ switch has only two settings, on and off.

11. Letters on the end of a filename that have a special meaning are a _____ .

12. _____ is an abbreviation for "frequently asked questions."

A. toggle

B. web site

C. FAQ

D. word processor

E. e-mail

F. icon

G. suffix

H. asterisk

I. pixels

J. data

K. MPEG

L. scroll bars

Answers appear on page 230.

GAME 19
Computer & Internet Word Match

Match each description to the correct term.

1. The device that you use to move a mouse pointer.

2. A disk that stores about 1.44 MB of memory.

3. A software program that you can use to view Web pages.

5. Rhymes with "mink" and you can click on it to view other Web pages.

5. A device with a ball that you can use to control a mouse pointer.

6. I saved the pictures of my summer vacation as _____ files.

7. What you use to print a document.

8. An acronym for "hypertext markup language."

9. An acronym for "graphical user interface."

10. A storage device that uses shiny disks to store data.

11. Something is wrong with this file. It may have a _____ .

12. What you use to view things on your computer.

A. monitor

B. floppy disk

C. mouse

D. browser

E. JPEG

F. HTML

G. virus

H. GUI

I. trackball

J. printer

K. CD-ROM

L. link

Answers appear on page 230.

GAME 20
Computer & Internet Word Match
Abbreviations from Chat, E-mail, and Usenet

Match each description to the correct term.

1. See you later.

2. back in a few minutes

3. Got to Go.

4. face to face

5. Long time no see.

6. in my humble opinion

7. Great minds think alike.

8. I am not a lawyer.

9. laughing out loud

10. people

11. thanks

12. Ta ta for now.

A. TNX

B. IMHO

C. CUL8R

D. IANAL

E. BBIAF

F. LOL

G. TTFN

H. G2G

I. F2F

J. GMTA

K. LTNS

L. PPL

Answers appear on page 230.

GAMES 21 TO 28
Computer & Internet Spelling Puzzles

In the following spelling puzzles, each term is either missing a letter, has one letter too many, or needs one letter changed. If a letter is missing or needs to be removed, then write that letter in the blank. If a letter needs to be changed, then write the correct letter in the blank. The letters in the blank spell an unknown term. What is the unknown term?

GAME 21

1. detug _____

2. dowrnload _____

3. scrill bar _____

4. netork _____

5. mirror ite _____

6. accss _____

7. dirsk _____

GAME 22

1. priner _____

2. esolution _____

3. virtual reility _____

4. databacse _____

5. formakt _____

6. Jabva _____

7. ddress _____

8. Word Wide Web _____

9. scannler _____

Answers appear on page 230.

GAMES 23 TO 24
Computer & Internet Spelling Puzzles

GAME 23

1. outut _____

2. memoy _____

3. mause _____

4. debuj _____

5. vius _____

6. uploed _____

7. moden _____

8. siulation _____

9. pexel _____

10. Intermet _____

11. imae _____

GAME 24

1. indow _____

2. excute _____

3. combpiler _____

4. morsph _____

5. monetor _____

6. acive _____

7. manu _____

Answers appear on page 230.

GAMES 25 TO 26
Computer & Internet Spelling Puzzles

GAME 25

1. edt _____

2. etwork _____

3. Interne _____

4. reeboot _____

5. tackball _____

6. acfronym _____

7. binry _____

8. kache _____

9. cookiee _____

GAME 26

1. mobuse _____

2. Jva _____

3. conokie _____

4. dowpload _____

5. srver _____

6. encypt _____

Answers appear on page 230.

GAME 27
Computer & Internet Spelling Puzzle

1. alimas   _____

2. hosit   _____

3. sicte   _____

4. tansistor   _____

5. fnt   _____

6. ort   _____

7. bromb   _____

8. dwn   _____

9. launh   _____

10. pixlate   _____

11. erver   _____

12. craeh   _____

13. fioeld   _____

14. encypt   _____

Answers appear on page 230.

GAME 28
Computer & Internet Spelling Puzzle

1. cht   _____

2. ibactive   _____

3. ste   _____

4. abmort   _____

5. sve   _____

6. palete   _____

7. actve   _____

8. fant   _____

9. meu   _____

Answers appear on page 230.

ANSWERS

GAME 1
Page 201

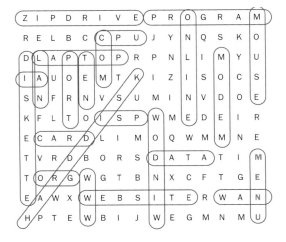

GAME 2
Page 202

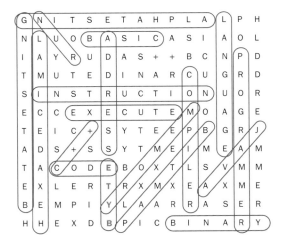

GAME 3
Page 203

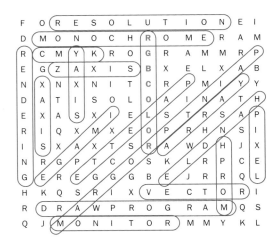

GAME 4
Page 204

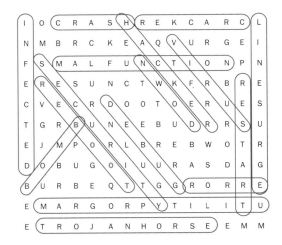

GAME 5
Page 205

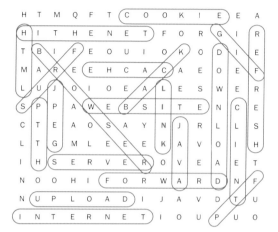

GAME 7
Page 207

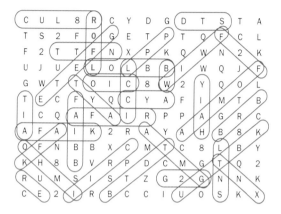

GAME 6
Page 206

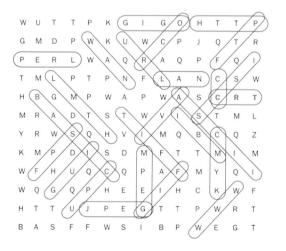

GAME 8
Page 208

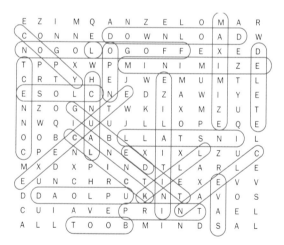

Answers

GAME 9
Page 209

1. PIXEL
2. VECTOR
3. RESOLUTION
4. MORPH
5. IMAGE
6. DRAW PROGRAM
7. PAINT PROGRAM
8. ARRAY
9. HANDLES

GAME 10
Page 210

1. BOMB
2. HACKER
3. RESTART
4. CRACKER
5. INFECTED
6. SECURITY
7. CRASH
8. LINE SURGE
9. TROJAN HORSE
10. DEBUG
11. MALFUNCTION
12. UTILITY PROGRAM
13. DOWN
14. VIRUS
15. ERROR

GAME 11
Page 211

1. BACK
2. LINK
3. BROWSER
4. HIT
5. REFRESH
6. CACHE
7. SERVER
8. CLIENT
9. SURE
10. COOKIE
11. INTERNET
12. DOWNLOAD
13. JAVA
14. UPLOAD
15. WEB SITE

GAME 12
Page 212

GAME 13
Page 213

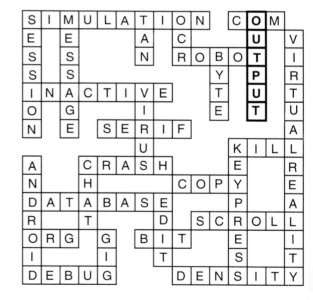

GAME 14
Page 214

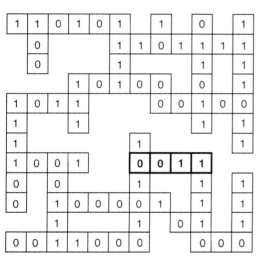

GAME 16
Page 216

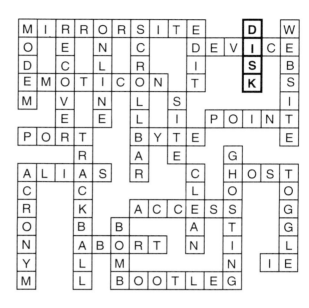

GAME 15
Page 215

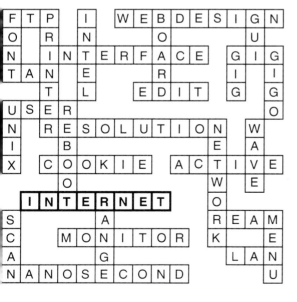

GAME 17
Page 217

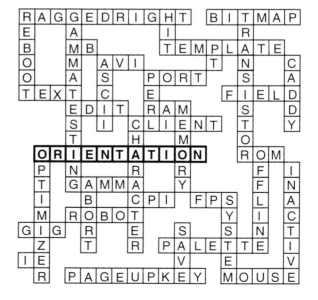

Answers

	GAME 18	GAME 19	GAME 20
1.	D	C	C
2.	E	B	E
3.	B	D	H
4.	J	L	I
5.	L	I	K
6.	H	E	B
7.	F	J	J
8.	K	F	D
9.	I	H	F
10.	A	K	L
11.	G	G	A
12.	C	A	G

GAME 21   **Page 221**
1. Change *t* to a *b*: debug; **2.** Remove an *r*: download; **3.** Change i to an *o*: scroll bar; **4.** Add a *w*: network; **5.** Add an *s*: mirror site; **6.** Add an *s*: access; **7.** Remove an *r*: disk; Unknown term: BROWSER

GAME 22   **Page 221**
1. Add a *t*: printer; **2.** Add an *r*: resolution; **3.** Change i to an *a*: virtual reality; **4.** Remove a *c*: database; **5.** Remove a *k*: format; **6.** Remove a *b*: Java; **7.** Add an *a*: address; **8.** Add an *l*: World Wide Web; **9.** Remove an *l*: scanner; Unknown term: TRACKBALL

GAME 23   **Page 222**
1. Add a *p*: output; **2.** Add an *r*: memory; **3.** Change *a* to an *o*: mouse; **4.** Change *j* to a *g*: debug; **5.** Add an *r*: virus; **6.** Change *e* to an *a*: upload; **7.** Change *n* to an *m*: modem; **8.** Add an *m*: simulation; **9.** Change *e* to an *i*: pixel; **10.** Change *m* to an *n*: Internet; **11.** Add a *g*: image; Unknown term: PROGRAMMING

GAME 24   **Page 222**
1. Add a *w*: window; **2.** Add an *e*: execute; **3.** Remove a *b*: compiler; **4.** Remove an *s:* morph; **5.** Change *e* to an *i*: monitor; **6.** Add a *t:* active; **7.** Change *a* to an *e:* menu; Unknown term: WEB SITE

GAME 25   **Page 223**
1. Add an *i*: edit; **2.** Add an *n*: network; **3.** Add a *t*: Internet; **4.** Remove an *e*: reboot; **5.** Add an *r*: trackball; **6.** Remove an *f*: acronym; **7.** Add an *a*: binary; **8.** Change *k* to a *c*: cache; **9.** Remove an *e*: cookie; Unknown term: INTERFACE

GAME 26   **Page 223**
1. Remove a *b*: mouse; **2.** Add an *a*: Java; **3.** Remove an *n*: cookie; **4.** Change *p* to an *n*: download; **5.** Add an *e*: server; **6.** Add an *r*: encrypt; Unknown term: BANNER

GAME 27   **Page 224**
1. Remove an *m*: alias; **2.** Remove an *i*: host; **3.** Remove a *c*: site; **4.** Add an *r*: transistor; **5.** Add an *o*: font; **6.** Add a *p*: port; **7.** Remove an *r*: bomb; **8.** Add an *o*: down; **9.** Add a *c*: launch; **10.** Add an *e*: pixelate; **11.** Add an *s*: server; **12.** Change *e* to an *s*: crash; **13.** Remove an *o*: field; **14.** Add an *r*: encrypt; Unknown term: MICROPROCESSOR

GAME 28   **Page 225**
1. Add an *a*: chat; **2.** Change *b* to an *n*: inactive; **3.** Add an *i*: site; **4.** Remove an *m*: abort; **5.** Add an *a*: save; **6.** Add a *t*: palette; **7.** Add an *i*: active; **8.** Change *a* to an *o*: font; **9.** Add an *n*: menu; Unknown term: ANIMATION